POSITIVE LEADERSHIP
How to build a winning team

Mike Pegg

MERCURY

First published in 1989 by Lifeskills Publishing Group
Published in paperback 1991
by Mercury Books
Gold Arrow Publications Ltd
862 Garratt Lane, London SW17 0NB

Set in Plantin by TecSet Ltd, Wallington, Surrey

**Printed and bound in Great Britain by
M & A Thomson Litho Ltd, East Kilbride, Scotland**

British Library Cataloguing in Publication Data

Pegg, Mike
    Positive Leadership
    1. Management, Leadership
    I. Title
    658. 4'092
ISBN 1–85251–185–0

CONTENTS

To Barrie and Mike – two great encouragers

ACKNOWLEDGEMENTS

My thanks to the following people who have made it possible to write this book.

Barrie Hopson and Mike Scally, managing directors of Lifeskills, who gave me the encouragement, time and freedom to complete the book.

Andy Clark, Liz Clarke, John Dodds and Ann Maxfield, my fellow consultants at Lifeskills, who accepted and supported my role as writer while they were out 'on the road'.

Christine Beels, Peter Gannon and everybody in the Lifeskills team who contributed to getting the book into print.

Karin Horowitz for all her hard work and patience in editing the script.

The people who granted me interviews and who gave feedback on the first manuscript. These include: David Miller of American Express; George Duncanson and Brian Spicer of British Airways; Arthur Ware of Century Oils Group; Jim Woodman of Federal Express (UK); Paul Bird and Neil Lewis of Grand Metropolitan; David Clutterbuck of The Item Group; Ken Birkby of Marks and Spencer; Roy Clarke of Pilkington Insulation; Tony Griffiths of 3M; Eric Nicoli and John Evans of United Biscuits; Fiona McGregor of Sun Alliance and Alec Dickson.

Bill and Gladys, my parents, and Berit, my wife, who are superb encouragers.

The good leaders I have known. They have provided the models, tools and results which I have been able to describe in this book.

INTRODUCTION

This book describes how to inspire your people to go from vision to action to results. We will be looking at many areas of life apart from business. These will include education, sport and other examples of teamwork.

Chris Bonington, for example, believes it is vital for the leader to have a crystal-clear goal. He had this in 1975 when selecting a group of talented mountaineers to climb the southwest face of Everest. After involving key people in creating the strategy, he made sure everybody knew their part in reaching the summit. Bonington kept his hands on the job, encouraged people to work hard and led the team to success. After two of his climbers, Doug Scott and Dougal Haston, had conquered the mountain, he wrote:

> Being a leader in industry, commerce or any other activity involving people requires much the same skills and techniques as being leader of an Everest expedition, only it is rather less dramatic and a lot less dangerous. But it need not be any less stimulating or, for that matter, less enjoyable.[1]

The leader may have a clear vision: but the hard part is to inspire people to make it happen. Liverpool Football Club have an outstanding track record in this respect. During the past 20 years they have made a habit of winning trophies such as the FA Cup, European Cup and League Championship. They have a far-sighted board who set clear goals, support the managerial team and recruit good players. Despite recent setbacks they remain hungry for success. Liverpool may or may not have heard of Kaizen – the Japanese concept of constant improvement – but they make it a way of life. This is a characteristic of many winning teams.

British Airways may have hit turbulent times in the early 1990s; but they had previously shown one way to tackle many of the challenges facing older-style companies. Lord King and Sir Colin Marshall took three steps towards creating a better future. First, the top team created their vision, communicated it to their people and got their commitment to reaching the goal. Second, the senior and middle managers – the implementers – learned how to provide positive leadership and build winning teams. Third, the frontliners were given the support and training they needed to give good service to the customers. British Airways improved their performance and profits. They also restored pride in the company and gained respect in the market.

People often take ten steps toward working well together, whether they are climbing a mountain, playing football or running an airline (see illustration). After reaching their goal, people must choose to develop or die. Some get stuck on the Titanic, others learn from what is happening in the world. Quick turn-around-time is vital, whether this means attitude turn-around-time or technical turn-around-time. Good teams reclarify their vision and tackle their next challenge.

This book offers a model you can use to guide your people to achieving positive results. It contains many examples from sport, as well as from work, because sport, like business, is an activity where leaders must inspire people to reach specific targets. It is also an area that I have worked with a great deal. Please take the ideas you like best from this book and use them to continue building a successful team. Good luck and enjoy the journey.

(Note: all the examples in this book are based on real people and events. In many cases their real names are used. In some cases names have been changed to respect their anonymity.)

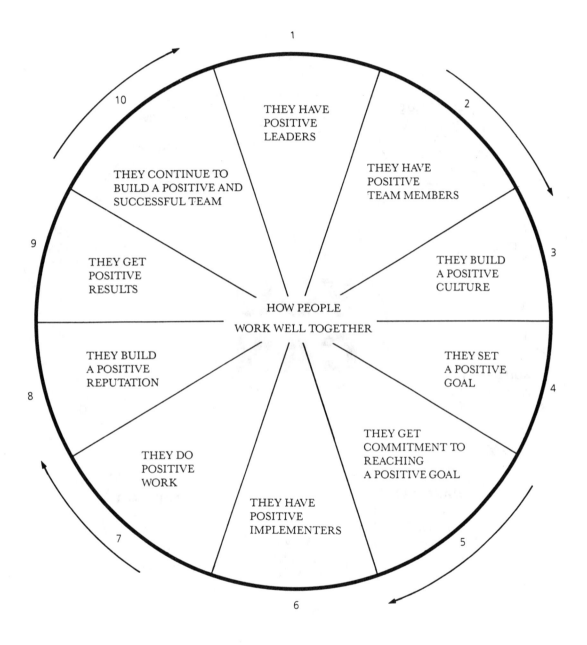

Chapter 1

HOW TO BE A POSITIVE LEADER

George Duncanson is an outstanding leader. He is the chief maintenance engineer for British Airways workshops and has the responsibility for leading 1,200 engineers. BA's corporate mission is 'to be the best', so his team aims 'to be the best airline maintenance workshops in the world'. How do they plan to reach this goal? They have chosen the strategy of introducing total quality management. During this book we will explore how George and his team have made this happen.

Mother Teresa is another outstanding leader. Apart from fighting hunger in India, she acts as a shining example for people throughout the world. She is a doer rather than a talker. Although she appears saint-like, she is also results-orientated. She frequently waits until the television cameras are whirring before asking local politicians to provide food, homes and money. The embarrassed officials have little choice but to say 'Yes'. Mother Teresa is a hope-giver who is building a better world.

Brian Clough is a controversial leader. After scoring goals for Middlesbrough and Sunderland, his playing days were cut short at the age of 29. His managerial career began at Hartlepool, before finding success at Derby County and Nottingham Forest. Some people call him an autocrat, but many players turn down tempting offers because they prefer to play for him. Clough has always produced attractive, disciplined and effective teams. He once blotted his own copy-book, however, by engaging in a public brawl after a cup match against Queens Park Rangers.

What have these people in common? Two things. First, they have many of the characteristics of compelling leaders who work to reach a clear goal. They have all the Cs. They are:

- charismatic

- caring

- committed

- crystal-clear
- communicators
- consistent
- creative
- competent
- courageous
- just a little bit crazy

They are crazy enough to believe that what they do can make a difference. They want to improve the football team, the airline workshops or the lot of people in Calcutta. They would feel even crazier if they felt they could not improve the world. Second, they build good leadership teams. While it's useful to be charismatic, competent and courageous, they need other people to share the load. Top teams in business, for example, often have people who fulfil the roles of visionary, people manager, implementer, financial manager and communicator. Brian Clough, for instance, has been most successful when he has built a good top team. Sam Longson was his chairman at Derby, where Peter Taylor was his assistant and Dave Mackay caried out his orders on the field. He created a similar set-up at Nottingham Forest, where he lifted the European Cup twice during the early 1980s. He did, however, taste failure at Leeds, where he inherited a culture which refused to accept his authority, his ideas and the people he imported. Forty-four days of in-fighting led to his being sacked by a club that went downhill for ten years. When Bobby Gould took over Wimbledon he rang Clough to ask his advice. The reply: 'Start by building a good backroom team.'

Before moving on to the nitty-gritty business of running a team, let's look at three steps you can take before becoming a leader. These are particularly vital if you are going to work for an organisation. People can hit trouble if they fail to consider these steps.

YOU CAN MAKE SURE YOU WANT TO BE A LEADER

The leader's role is both rewarding and lonely. George Duncanson, for example, has risen through the ranks and knows all the risks. A typical engineering apprentice, he was 'one of the lads' who worked on the shop floor and did not dream of becoming a manager. He was in his mid-30s before he made several life decisions. He decided to

'Start by building a good backroom team.'
Brian Clough

give everything he could to British Airways, to educate himself as a leader and to perform high quality work. He then rose like a rocket to become the chief maintenance engineer. George accepts both the pluses and the minuses of the job. He loves the challenges.

Will you accept the whole leadership package? Imagine, for example, that you are the chief executive for a major international airline. Let's look at a few points on each side of the equation.

The possible pluses

- You have the chance to run a famous company.

- You have the chance to compete in the international market.

- You have a stimulating job, money and status.

- You have the opportunity to use your business skills.

- You have the chance to create an exciting vision.

- You have the power to make things happen.

- You have many excellent managers.

- You have a highly skilled work-force.

- You have the challenge of being judged by your results.

- You have great rewards if you build a successful company.

The possible minuses

- You have inherited an old-style company.

- You have only as much freedom as the board give you.

- You have to live with the job 24 hours a day.

- You have to rely on other people to implement your ideas.

- You have to go to bed each night knowing that an aircraft could crash – and that you will have to face the press in the morning.

- You have to live with the possibility of industrial disputes.

- You have to accept that your employees will probably respect you, rather than like you.

- You have a highly competitive market in the airline business.

- You have the chance of becoming a scapegoat if things go wrong.

- You have to accept that there will be great demands on your family.

Look at your own leadership job and try the exercise below. This invites you to list both the pluses and the minuses involved in your work. Build on the good parts and make a strategy for dealing with the difficult parts. Then decide if you want to accept the whole package.

THE LEADERSHIP PACKAGE

Look at your own leadership job and list all the possible pluses and minuses. Apart from the obvious things, try to find factors that you may not have considered before.

Give yourself a full picture.

Pluses	Minuses
• Run own Company	• Financial worries
• Be creative with	• Long hours 24hrs
• Travel	• Must be a leader
• Meet people	• It's my responsibility
• Become respected	• Must manage
• DTI	• Recession hit
• Freedom (?)	• Personal time cut
• It's mine	• Pauline loses out
• My work	• Mental/physical damage of Stress
• Power (?)	
• Chairoloead	
• Management.	

Build on the good parts and make a strategy for dealing with the difficult parts. You can then decide if you want to accept the whole package.

YOU CAN WORK FOR AN ORGANISATION YOU BELIEVE IN

Good leaders follow their life philosophy. Mother Teresa draws strength from Christianity, other leaders are motivated by other basic beliefs. Many people join companies such as Johnson & Johnson, United Biscuits and J Sainsbury because they stand for something. They have a written credo or a set of values that attract dedicated people. More importantly, they follow these guidelines even in their darkest hours. People are proud to translate their beliefs into actions. The same principle applies whether you are working in education, business or government. I can illustrate this with one of my own experiences from sport. In August 1984 two Swedish football clubs invited me to lead their youth development programmes. I chose to join the Second Division team which had a record of treating its employees well and playing attractive football. Why? They had a clear goal and I admired the way they put their ideals into practice.

'We want you to make our youth team the best in Sweden,' said the chairman of Enköping Sports Klubb. 'At the moment we are rated around number 120. We want to become number one by 1987. Why? Because developing our own talent is the only way we can compete with the big city clubs.'

Before taking the job, however, I had to make sure we had the resources to reach the target. This brings us to the third step.

YOU CAN MAKE A CLEAR CONTRACT WITH THE ORGANISATION

People can be so flattered by being offered a leadership position that they neglect to get the right back-up. Whatever kind of team you are leading – whether it is in a school, organisation or company – here are some points to consider.

You can clarify your vision for the team

Start by clarifying your own picture of what you want to achieve. Enköping Sports Klubb, for example, wanted their youth team to be the best in Sweden. Although winning is great, I believe there is more to football: it must be joyful and offer people golden memories. We must help the young people to grow as players and as individuals. The aim would be 'success with style' both on and off the field. If the club and I could not agree on this vision, there was little point in taking the job. My first move was to watch all the club's players aged between 14 and 16 who would form the basis of the 1987 team. Successful football teams need players who have a positive attitude. They also need at least nine quality players and four match-winners. After studying the youngsters, it was obvious I would have to sign seven new players. There was one complication: Swedish football clubs have a social responsibility and aim to give all young people the chance to play football. By 1987 we would have a pool of twenty-six 16 to 18 year olds, so I decided to create two teams. One elite team and one for players of average ability.

You can agree with your bosses on the vision for your team

Meet your boss and write down three concrete goals for your team. You are, after all, employed by the organisation to do a job: whether you are working for Marks and Spencer, Rolls Royce or the British government. They are the people who pay your wages. If you cannot agree on common goals, then look elsewhere to do creative work.

The Board of Enköping Sports Klubb, for example, said they agreed with the vision and asked me to outline my action plan. I explained:

'The first year will be spent on two things: developing an attractive playing style and getting visible results. I will build a managerial team of three people and bring in three good players to change the team's chemistry. Everybody will work hard to impress us during the first few weeks because they aim to win their places in the team. The negative players will return to their old habits after one month. We will then be fair but tough: we will ask whether or not they want to play for us. We will then keep the players we want to keep. The team will finish in the top three in our league and win a medal in one of the cup competitions. The players will feel successful. Five extra players will be required before the second season. We will win our league title and move into the top thirty in Sweden. Tangible results will arrive in the shape of winning more trophies. The third year will be the hardest. Three new players will be needed if we are to compete at the highest level. The team will move into the top ten in Sweden and win more cups. This is the most I can promise. What do you think?'

The Board liked what they heard, but then came the trickiest part. I needed their help to reach the target. This brings us to the next step.

You can ask for the support you need to do the job

Your employers may ask you to climb Everest. If so, dare to say: 'Give me the back-up and I will produce the results'. What if they refuse? You may have to agree on simply setting up the base camp or, alternatively, climbing the Matterhorn or Ben Nevis. Get the resources you need to do the job.

Enköping Sports Klubb committed themselves to the Youth Programme's aim of 'success with style'. They budgeted money to pay the managerial team, recruit new players and run two teams. They also promised support in dealing with any problem players. More importantly, they gave us the freedom to reach the goals in our own way. (What happened? Two years later I took a job in England and chose my own successor at the club. The youth team had by then reached the top 30. They ended the 1987 season as the number eight club in Sweden.)

So much for the preliminaries: let's get on to the nitty-gritty business. What can you actually do as a leader? Here are ten steps you can take to build a successful team.

1: YOU CAN BUILD A POSITIVE LEADERSHIP TEAM

Start by building a winning team at the top. Why? Because no one person has all the qualities needed to be a leader in today's world. There are very few perfect leaders. Lee Iacocca, for example, chose this route when taking over at Chrysler. Apart from recruiting talent from within the company, he reached out to his old network. 'There was one pool of people who had a body of experience and proven ability that was going to waste', he writes in his autobiography, 'they were retired Ford executives. I needed to pick their brains and use their street smarts to get things organised'.[1]

Top teams often gather together people who fulfil the following roles. It is not necessary to have five people, it can be two or three, but all the qualities are needed. They need:

Your employers may ask you to climb Everest. If so, dare to say: 'Give me the back-up and I will produce the results'.

A visionary

~~BRIAN~~ TERRY

Someone who sees what can be achieved and crystallises the vision. This kind of leader also has the ability to see opportunities within a crisis. They start from their destination, work backwards and clarify the strategy. They tend to be more concerned with long-term goals, rather than short-term feelings. He or she is both totally supportive and totally demanding.

A people manager

TIM

Someone who is an encourager, unifier and motivator. The figure-head may be wonderful at leading the column, but someone must manage the troops and raise morale. The people manager clarifies the messages coming from the top team, 'listens downwards' and, when necessary, heals hurt feelings. They are seen as a caring person, but can also inspire staff to do their best for the organisation.

An implementer

COLIN

Someone who translates the beautiful vision into action and achieves positive results. When Apple Computers hit stormy weather, for example, John Sculley recruited several old hands who had mastered the basics. They charted a rescue course, turned things around and steered the company to safer waters. Visionaries know what must be done: implementers know how to get things done.

A financial manager

Melanie

Someone who keeps everybody's feet on the ground. They must be a positive stopper who educates people to spend money wisely. Financial managers have an important role to play in the future because staff will be asked to deliver better quality at lower cost. Budget problems, however, are often a symptom of other difficulties. Management must tackle the real problem, rather than blindly choosing cost-cutting, otherwise they may cut out the heart of the company.

> *Visionaries know what must be done: implementers know how to get things done.*

A communicator

Someone who reaches people both inside and outside the organisation. They must start by winning the hearts and minds of their own staff. The communicator must also keep in touch with the marketing team to ensure they reach the right target group and get the right results. They must ensure the organisation builds a good reputation so they continue to attract talented people.

What about your own top team? Try rating yourselves in the exercise below. If you are hopeless people managers, for example, give yourselves 0. If you are superb, give yourselves 9 or 10. You may also wish to check this with your staff. Anything below 7 is a danger signal, but, whatever the rating, ask yourselves: 'How can we improve as people managers?'

THE POSITIVE LEADERSHIP TEAM

Look at your top team and rate yourselves on a scale from 0 to 10 in the following areas. You can also rate how you think your employees see you – or even get them to do this if you wish.

	How we rate ourselves 0–10	How we think others rate us 0–10
Vision	3	
People management	4	
Implementation	8	
Financial management	6 | 7	
Communication: internal	4	
external	4	.

What skills do you have? What skills do you need to develop? What skills do you have to bring into your team? How can you do this? When? Make a concrete action plan for building an even better top team.

Leaders can offer their people the three Ss: security, specific goals and success. I can illustrate this by comparing the responses of two television manufacturers during the stock market crash of October 1987. Company A was known for its good leadership, excellent

> *Management must tackle the real problem, rather than blindly choosing cost-cutting, otherwise they may cut out the heart of the company.*

quality and far-sighted planning. Company B was known for its poor leadership, bad quality and fire-fighting.

You can offer people security

Leaders can offer people 80% security and 20% challenge. Many workers have mortgages, children and personal ambitions, so they look for certainty. Some leaders are blind to this because they are frequently motivated by challenges. Try to offer your staff the right balance. Job security is a non-starter, but you can offer people other kinds of certainty.

Company A
The top team took charge immediately after the October Crash. They called the whole staff together, reassured them the company was healthy and promised to create a win/win strategy. Apart from holding regular staff briefings, several top managers ate lunch in the restaurant each day. Managers were visible and willing to talk with any worried employees.

Company B
The top team retreated into their bunker to discuss long-term strategy. They emerged one month later to fire 50 workers from the television assembly lines. Rumours spread around the factory as to who would be the next victims. The only messages coming from the top team were: 'Cost-cutting, cost-cutting, cost-cutting.'

You can offer people specific goals

People like to have clear goals: this is especially true during change, challenge and crisis. Winston Churchill, for example, knew the value of providing both short-term and long-term targets during the Second World War. People feel better if they know where they are going.

Company A
The top team called the staff together after one month and outlined their new plans for the next year. The company's high share of the television market was based on offering good quality at a price

comparable to its Asian competitors. The best way forward, they believed, was to improve their quality management. The top team acted as models and resolved to improve their people management. They aimed to keep the staff informed and make better use of their know-how. The assembly staff were asked to improve their products and practices, while the sales department were asked to improve their 'packaging', the way they presented the product to the customer. Nobody would be laid off. Providing they worked together as a team, the company would reach its financial targets.

Company B
The middle managers emerged each week to conduct the 'Friday executions'. The skilled staff who weren't sacked started to look for jobs elsewhere in the electrical industry. Two months later the top team reappeared with news of a take-over which would retain the company's name. No promises about job security or financial prospects – that would depend on the new owners.

You can offer people success

Good leaders focus on a realistic hope. They are honest, explain the strategy and inspire people to tackle the challenge. They lead by example, ask for 100% effort and explain the benefits. They have a clear action plan and fighting spirit which is transmitted to other people. Leaders cannot guarantee success. They can promise, however, that people who do their best are more likely to succeed.

Company A
The top team said that providing quality at low cost was a key factor in the television market. Customer research revealed this to be their most effective selling strategy during the next two years. Christmas orders were up on last year and there was every prospect of a successful future. Staff would be given all the support they needed to deliver the goods. The top team repeated they would continue with their plans to introduce a profit-sharing scheme during the next financial year.

Company B
The top team were already packing their bags, so they couldn't promise success. One or two were sitting in deserted offices waiting

> *Leaders can offer people 80% security and 20% challenge.*

for the new owners to announce their plans. Rumour had it that all the television sets would be assembled in Asia and shipped over to the UK. The brand name would live on, but there would be little work for the local staff. It was a sad end for the company.

Leaders are important; but other people often do the actual work. This brings us to the second step towards building a successful team.

2: YOU CAN HAVE POSITIVE TEAM MEMBERS

Leaders are only as good as their people. Michael Checkland, director general of the BBC, depends on the telephonists, the backroom technicians and the newsreaders, such as Michael Buerk. His performance will be judged by the quality of their work. Leaders have to attract, develop and keep good people.

You want people who are positive

Eric Nicoli, managing director of United Biscuits Brands, for example, looks for three characteristics when selecting people. They need to be talented, honest and have a sense of humour. UB Brands have an enthusiastic and hard-working culture, but they are not alone. Providing the leaders build a good atmosphere, virtually all of their people will do a fair day's work for a fair day's pay.

Konosuke Matsushita underlines this point in his book *Not for bread alone*. He says:

> Everyone is an asset . . . I would say that a manager ought to give at least 70% of his attention to the positive qualities of his subordinates; 30% is enough for those points that need improvement or changing. Employees, for their part, should try to see the strong points in their managers as much as possible. Positive attitudes on both sides will augment the productivity of the team, and contribute to the personal growth of all concerned.[2]

You want people who are professional

Sue Lawley, for instance, overcame a much publicised studio invasion in 1988 and continued to read the *Six O'Clock News*. She researches her subjects properly, whether hosting a chat show or *Desert Island Discs*. She can be relied on to do an excellent job.

Leaders must invest in training to enable their staff to continue to do good work. The BBC are going beyond offering technical training and have budgeted for courses in management skills, career management and performance management. Care should be taken when introducing such training, however, because people must 'own' the knowledge if they are going to use it. Leaders who tackle this challenge properly will equip their staff to continue to do professional work.

You want people who are performers

Michael Buerk, for example, has the ability to bring a story to life. His report about the Ethiopian famine brought the tragedy into viewers' living rooms and spurred Bob Geldof to set up Band Aid. He is a superb communicator: whether reading the news or presenting 'Nature'. He has a quality check in his guts and always does his best.

Many companies are now introducing performance management systems to help people to clarify and reach their goals. Programmes such as these must meet four conditions if they are to succeed. First, they must be introduced properly into the organisation. Second, they must be simple and easy to understand. Third, they must be seen as a good experience for almost everybody. Fourth, they must lead to positive results for the people and the organisation. We will be exploring this area further in Chapter Six.

3: YOU CAN BUILD A POSITIVE CULTURE

Marvin Bower defines culture as 'The way we do things around here'[3]. IBM's culture, for example, hits you as soon as you enter the building. Everything is big, clean and tidy. People are polite, sociable and professional. John Akers, their chief executive, has defined what is missing: it is fire, hunger and entrepreneurship. Middle managers are now being urged to stop pushing paper and get out to meet the customers. IBM are returning to the basics that made them successful.

There are two extreme kinds of culture. Old organisations are often based on roles and power. They have military-like hierarchies in which orders are passed down to people who have strict roles. Staff have clear status, certain powers and follow the rules. Obedience is rewarded and mistakes are punished. Creativity is stifled. Procedures come first and customers come last. Frontliners answer

> *Leaders are only as good as their people.*

complaints by saying: 'The company's policy is not to . . . ' The organisation looks inward and becomes complacent.

New organisations are based on support and achievement. The top team clarify their vision, communicate it to their people and get their commitment. They have few layers of management, encourage dialogue goal-setting and expect people to be entrepreneurial. Staff are given the support they need and are willing to be judged by their results. Customers come first because they pay people's wages. Frontliners answer complaints by saying: 'We will fix it.' The organisation looks outward and continues to improve.

Leaders must ensure their cultures have the right values and vision. People will then have the vitality to work hard and achieve visible results. Healthy culture are based on the three Es: encouragement, enterprise and excellence. Encouragement must be the first building block, whether you are building a team, company or country; otherwise there will be some winners and lots of losers. People can then be asked to take initiatives and develop in a spirit of enterprise. The next step is to urge people to go for excellence. Providing they have been given the support they need, people will try to do their best. Healthy cultures are those where the vast majority of people feel like winners.

4: YOU CAN SET A POSITIVE GOAL

Chris Bonington's team had a clear goal in 1975: 'We want to climb Everest by the southwest face'. Spurred on by this picture, people combined their talents to overcome the challenge. Scott and Haston reached the summit, but their triumph was the result of teamwork. The expedition would have been embarrassed to discover they had climbed K2 by mistake.

Leaders must ensure their team are climbing the right mountain. How? Start by defining your strengths, weaknesses, opportunities and threats. Define your target group and find out what they want. Build on your strengths and match these to the market opportunities. Clarify your action plan for reaching the goal. Inspire your people to want to reach the summit. Then work hard. Some teams unfortunately spend a lot of energy climbing the wrong mountain. Mountaineers often plan their expeditions by looking at the summit and working backwards, rather than by gazing at the twig lying at their feet. Repeat this process several times: by yourself, with your top team and with people at various levels in the organisation. You will already have a provisional vision for your team, but involve key people in the goal-setting: the 'What? Why? and When?' Further down in the organisation you can involve people in developing their part of the strategy and action plan. They must be able to 'own' the 'How' in order to make it happen. Ask yourselves these questions:

- What is the result we want to achieve?

- Why do we want to achieve this result?

- How can we do our best to achieve this result?

- When do we want to achieve this result?

- What will tell us we have achieved this result?

What about language? Does it matter if you talk about vision, mission or goal? Some people, for instance, find the word 'vision' to be too trendy. As David Hancock, then managing director of Apple's British company, once said:

> The other way is to set a destiny and get your people to buy into it. Vision is an incredibly misused word . . . a Hollywood word in business. But if you give people the freedom and means to reach their destiny they almost always will.[4]

The ForeSight Group, who are based in Sweden, offered another point of view in their second Quarterly Newsletter in 1988. In an article entitled 'The difference between a mission and a vision', they wrote:

> A mission is a long-term reason for the existence of your organisation or project. What is the purpose of your organisation? How do you make yourselves useful? These are key elements in the time transcending mission. In short, a mission is very long-term and describes a purpose. A vision is a clear description of a desired state at a particular moment in time. President John F Kennedy said the United States would put a man on the moon and return him safely to earth before the end of the 1960s. This was a clear and compelling vision which was accomplished. But some believe the mission of NASA was never clear after the Apollo lunar landing programme, resulting in many of the problems the agency has experienced in more recent years.[5]

Leaders such as David Hancock and Chris Bonington may use different words, but the key is to inspire people to want to reach the goal. This brings us to the next step.

5: YOU CAN GET COMMITMENT TO REACHING A POSITIVE GOAL

Katerina faced a challenge. At 42 she had fulfilled her ambition to become the chief executive of a famous theatre in Denmark. She took over a theatre, however, which had lost direction, had few funds and had a discontented staff. Actors and technicians harked back to the 1960s and '70s when political theatre was popular and the state supplied money. The '80s brought diminishing audiences who did not want to be harangued about being capitalists. The previous chief executive became sandwiched between the staff who wanted to keep their integrity and the city officials who threatened to withdraw funds.

Katerina was hired to clean up the mess. She had to start by winning the hearts of the staff because they were the people who actually did the work in the theatre. Financial pressures meant she also had to balance the books. Katerina didn't see money as a big problem: she had a clear vision for success. The hard part was to give the staff a sense of 'ownership' in developing the goal-setting and strategy. She handled this by getting everybody involved in a customer survey.

The entire staff interviewed potential audiences about what would attract them to the theatre. They emerged from their artistic ghetto to see what was happening in the outside world. Audience research showed that many people wanted to attend the theatre, but they were divided into two segments. Some wanted entertainment, others wanted thought-provoking plays. Katerina knew this before conducting the survey, but it was necessary in order to get the staff on board. While keeping their integrity, they must become more customer oriented, otherwise the theatre would close. She gave the staff one month to digest the survey. She then presented her vision of 'Two Theatres'. The main auditorium would offer mainstream entertainment, receive business sponsorship and stage popular plays and musicals. The first production would be 'Guys and Dolls'. Part of the sponsorship deal would include using a percentage of the money to create a 300-seat theatre. This would stage experimental work and alternative plays. Architects were ready to draw up plans for converting storage space and rehearsal rooms. A dance studio and wine bar would be added to provide extra income.

Katerina outlined the pluses. Staff would retain their jobs, be able to do work they preferred and develop as professionals. Customers could choose entertainment or thought-provoking plays. City officials would have less of a financial burden. Sponsors would have their names associated with high quality work. The theatre would survive, build a good reputation and attract future sponsorship. Minuses were equally obvious. Staff must find new rehearsal rooms and storage space. They might also feel they were sacrificing their political traditions and selling out to business. Katerina said they must make their own individual decisions on this issue. She believed, however, that there was little alternative to becoming money conscious. Sponsors might also withdraw at some stage. If the staff created a successful theatre, however, there would be a queue of potential backers.

'What do you think?' asked Katerina. She listened for half an hour to people discussing the pros and cons. The whole staff had been involved in the survey, however, so they understood the customers' expectations and the financial pressures on the theatre. The few criticisms which emerged were met by other group members asking, 'What do you suggest as an alternative?' The whole staff team eventually agreed on building 'Two Theatres'. Katerina presented a short-term action plan. She outlined the areas that staff could influence, then asked them to develop ideas for production over the next three years. One team focused on the main auditorium; another on the small theatre. They were asked to report back within a week in order to maintain the momentum. People had to see they could make a difference, so she promised to include some of their suggestions in the final programme.

Encouragement, commitment and achievement: these are three key steps in team building. Katerina had taken her staff through the first two steps. She spent time getting to know people, then showed what was happening in the world. She involved staff in this process so they could gain a sense of 'ownership'. She presented a positive vision, described the benefits and was honest about the costs. She then gave people the chance to discuss the ideas. She followed up by involving them in creating part of the strategy and getting an early visible success. Katerina had managed to win her people and get their commitment to reaching the goal. They must now deliver the results.

6: YOU CAN HAVE POSITIVE IMPLEMENTERS

Visionaries know what needs to be done; implementers know how to get things done. The quality of a company often depends on the quality of its implementers. They are the people who must translate the beautiful visions into nitty-gritty actions. They are the ones who will make things happen.

> *Healthy cultures are based on the three Es: encouragement, enterprise and excellence.*

George Duncanson had to decide how to introduce total quality management (TQM) into the BA workshops. Should it be managed by the top team? Should he use the management structure and rely on the cascade system? Should he set up an implementation team who would take responsibility for running the programme? George chose the last option. He set up a team who worked full time on introducing TQM into the workshops. The top team provided constant back-up and met the implementation team each week to monitor their progress.

Implementation teams need people who have 'street credibility'. George made sure they were respected by other engineers, knew their way about the system and believed in TQM. He invited Brian Spicer, a superintendent, to lead the programme. A superb integrator, Brian was good at listening to people, achieving consensus and putting ideas into practice. Together with the top team, he then selected five people who complemented each other. They were skilled at internal marketing, running courses and producing visible results.

George involved the team in producing the vision for BA workshops. They planned 'to be the best' in their chosen field and TQM was the strategy. Having the vision was easy: it was harder to translate it into action. They must win their own people, create a feeling of ownership and get some early success signals. The top team began by living the TQM message. They improved their own people management and provided the necessary support. Brian Spicer's team broke down the vision into a concrete action plan and launched the strategy. They created a feeling of 'ownership'. Brian's team asked their fellow engineers to submit suggestions for improving their back-home work-place. BA engineers are proud professionals who believe quality is the best way to compete against other airlines. They introduced TQM into their daily work and achieved visible results. George began the process, but Brian's team and the engineers delivered the results. Top teams are only as good as their implementers.

7: YOU CAN MAKE SURE PEOPLE DO POSITIVE WORK

Business leaders are responsible for everything produced by their company. Imagine, for example, that you have been invited to run Dillons bookshop in London, which is one of the best in the country. Terry Maher, the chairman, and the rest of the management are ambitious. They plan to make Dillons the best bookshop in the

> *Top teams are only as good as their implementers.*

world. Charged with implementing this vision, you cannot be everywhere at once. You must rely on your managers and front-liners. Apart from developing the right business strategy, how can you inspire your staff to *want* to perform excellent work? One way is to introduce a quality programme into the bookshop. How can you start? Live the message, lead by example and establish your credibility. Start by improving your own people management. Ask your people how the company can make better use of their knowledge, talents and ideas. Introduce many of their suggestions. Why? Quality programmes must have commitment from the top. They must also give people a sense of 'ownership' and provide quick successes. What next? You can create an implementation team who introduce 'Kaizen' into Dillons. What areas can they tackle? Two of the directors of Lifeskills, Barrie Hopson and Mike Scally, for example, believe companies can develop by focusing on the four Ps: their products, people skills, practices and packaging.[6] (Some aspects of your work may not fit into this model, but it provides a good starting point.) The implementation team can co-ordinate people's suggestions in each of the four categories.

Your products

Dillons have over five miles of bookshelves which cover virtually every subject. They also have a second-hand department for buffs who love to find bargains. How can you improve your products? Before answering this question, however, it is vital to clarify your vision. Do you want to be the best bookshop in the world or simply aim for a certain market segment? Who are your target group? Find out what your customers *really* want and meet their requirements. You may choose to offer a wider selection of books, be more selective or enlarge one or two sections.

Your people skills

Dillons' reputation will be shaped by the quality of its people. Start by asking the managers to suggest ways they can be even better team leaders. People react badly to finger-pointing, so ask them to produce their own answers. Then ask the frontliners to suggest ways they can provide even better service during the 'moments of truth', the times when they have direct contact with the customers. Give everybody the support and training they need to improve their people skills.

*Live the message,
lead by example
and establish
your credibility.*

Your practices

Start with your customer practices. How can you continue to put the customer first rather than last? One famous bookshop, for example, used to induce migraine with its archaic paying system. Purchasers were forced to queue three times to buy a book: first to present the book to an assistant and receive a paying order; then to present this note to the cashier; finally to return and collect the prize. Buying a book from another section called for repeating the torture. Dillons don't make this mistake, but can you make it even easier to buy books? Can you improve any of your other customer practices? Look at your work practices. How can you make things easier for the staff and more effective for the company (but not at the expense of the customer)? Moving a filing cabinet, for example, can be a quality improvement if it saves time, shoe leather and energy. The bookshop staff will be able to suggest at least 100 ways to improve your work practices.

Your packaging

The way you present your products can provide a competitive edge over other bookshops. Can the windows be more eye-catching? Can you improve the book displays? Can you give the staff attractive uniforms? Can you pin up book reviews? Can you provide seats for browsing? Can you have a café with newspapers and journals? Can you offer a gift-wrapping service? Can you give away bookmarks with each purchase? Can you produce your own free guide to books? Will these measures be cost effective? How can you improve your packaging?

Leaders are paid to ensure their people do good work. Introducing a quality programme is one way to achieve this result. The bookshop staff would find many ways to improve the four Ps. The implementation team would then co-ordinate the ideas, publicise success stories and launch the next phase. The High Street is competitive and today's luxury becomes tomorrow's expectation. Kaizen must become a way of life in any company which aims to build a good reputation.

8: YOU CAN BUILD A POSITIVE REPUTATION

Maybe it sounds idealistic; but I believe companies gain by caring for their people, products, profits, public duties and planet. Caring for the first three brings obvious benefits; but what's the value in being a good corporate citizen? Chapter Eight will focus on the global issues; for the moment, however, let's think locally.

Tad Tuleja describes many of the social initiatives taken by American companies in his book *Beyond the Bottom Line*. Xerox, for example, have encouraged their people to set up Community Involvement Teams. They do, however, set certain conditions. The projects they tackle should have the potential for employee involvement and be manageable within a given time frame. They should have clear objectives and meet a current need within the community. Some examples of their work have been:

- In Jefferson City, Missouri, Xerox volunteers worked with the local optimist club and the police and fire departments to produce a one-day 'traffic safety clinic' – complete with a miniature safety city – for children in the area.

- In Albany, New York, Xerox technical reps set up an ongoing Saturday morning course in electricity and physics at a school for boys with social adjustment problems.

- In 1980, an Atlanta XCIP began rebuilding a ghetto church that had been destroyed by fire. Working weekends under the guidance of a local carpenter, they finished the project in 1983.

- Xerox volunteers in Middletown, Connecticut handled publicity and promotion for a fund-raising drive that brought in $50,000 for a shelter for the homeless.

- In Los Angeles, XCIP people from eight company locations trained handicapped students in computer literacy and other job skills.

Xerox employees also have the chance to take part in the social service leave programme which began in 1971. This allows people to take time off from their jobs to make a contribution to the community for between a month to a year. People choose their own projects and work on them at full pay. Marion Whipple, the manager in charge of such programmes, believes this creates a win/win situation. Both the company and the community benefit:

> Of course we get some PR out of these programmes, but that's not our primary intent. We recognise that we have a social responsibility as well as a business responsibility. We want the communities where we do business to know that we're not there

simply to take something out, but to put something back. And we feel our employees do that for us.[7]

The company also gets back a 'better employee': 'They've learned new interpersonal skills, they know what it's like in other organisations, they're better able to deal with people. That's a big gain for the company.'

What about British companies? United Biscuits were one of many firms that raised funds for the Great Ormond Street Hospital. National Westminster Bank have promised a minimum of £3m in sponsorship for the World Wide Fund for Nature. British Airways have become a founding member of the Save the Children Fund's corporate membership scheme and aim to raise £300,000 over the next three years. Kwik-Fit offered child safety seats for cars and refunded the discounted price when the child had outgrown the seat. Sir Hector Laing, former chairman of United Biscuits, and Sir Mark Weinberg of Allied Dunbar, have become driving forces behind a UK version of the 'Per cent' Club. One hundred and twenty of the top 200 companies have now committed themselves to putting aside 0.5% of their pre-tax profits for social spending. Many UK companies – such as Rowntrees, Tesco and Forte – have a fine track record of sponsoring causes in the community. They find this creates good will and, as a side effect, it may even improve the bottom line.

9: YOU CAN GET POSITIVE RESULTS

Leaders are like airline pilots: they must keep their hands on the job and guide the team to success. Delegation is one thing, abdication is another. Too many 'aircraft' have crash landed because the 'captain' took his or her hands off the controls. The chief steward, for example, is qualified to welcome passengers, serve the food and motivate the cabin staff, but not qualified to fly the plane. Leaders must educate people by using delegation, but they must not use this as an excuse for slipping away into more enticing pursuits. The airline pilot, and leader, is paid to finish the job properly.

Ron Dennis, for example, has a superb track record in the world of motor racing as leader of the successful McLaren team. One of his sponsors said:

Two things impressed me about Ron. The first was his conviction that nothing was impossible. The second was his remarkable clarity of vision. Most people tend to think about next

> *Too many 'aircraft' have crash landed because the 'captain' took his or her hands off the controls.*

weekend, the next race, or perhaps the next season. In Ron's case it was about the next two, five, even ten years. Everything you see in the McLaren pit today, the whole infrastructure, was clearly positioned in his mind back in the early 1970s.[8]

Dennis pays enormous attention to detail. John Blunsden, motor racing correspondent of *The Times*, says the McLaren pit area looks like an exhibition stand. Floors are swept minutes after every practice session, newly laundered clothes are worn each day and people have new shoes for each race meeting. Framed pictures in the hospitality unit are constantly changed to record the latest successes and fresh flowers match the team colours. Dennis is around to make sure that these things happen.

'His ability to motivate people is one of his greatest strengths' says Richard West, his contracts co-ordinator. 'He engenders a tremendous team spirit, even though he is a hard task master. He's a perfectionist who lays down the most exacting standards of personal performance in every detail, but he's instilled in everyone the idea that McLaren isn't his team, it's *their* team. Therefore, his way of doing things should be their way because that's the only way if you're going to be the best.'[9]

Business leaders ensure their people focus on the 3Rs. They must create the right relationships, results and repeat business. Dennis has done this for McLaren in motor sports. He has built a good team of mechanics, drivers and backers; won championships; and continued to attract sponsors. He has led his team to achieving excellent results.

10: YOU CAN CONTINUE TO BUILD A POSITIVE TEAM

You can choose to develop or die. The British motor-cycle industry failed to respond to the Japanese challenge in the 1950s and almost collapsed. The trade union movement faces difficulties as it attempts to develop a fresh role in the 1990s. The Soviet Union made a half-hearted attempt at privatisation to ensure it was equipped to tackle the 21st century. Organisations must sometimes make risky decisions to stay ahead of the game.

George Duncanson realised BA workshops must anticipate change to stay ahead of their competitors. 'What competitors?', you may ask. British Airways pays its 1,200 engineers to keep the airline's planes in the air. The company does, however, ask for reliable and cost effective service. What would happen if there was a protracted strike? What would happen if sub-contractors showed they could service the planes more cheaply? 'Surely BA would stick with their own staff', you might say. Probably, but a lot of changes have taken place during the last ten years. Who knows what will happen when deregulation reaches the airlines? George is making sure that workshops stay ahead of the changes. They offer value for money to the company and do sub-contract work by servicing planes for other airlines. This brings in extra revenue and helps to safeguard their future.

'There's nothing more dangerous than yesterday's success' is a phrase often used by leaders. Winning teams also face challenges if they want to develop. West Indian cricket, for example, has based its triumphs on attacking batting and hostile fast bowling. Great players like Gary Sobers, Clive Lloyd and Wes Hall have given way to Viv Richards, Geoffrey Dujon and Malcolm Marshall. They also blooded several promising young players during their 1988 tour of England. The West Indies won the series 4-0 and laid the foundations for the future. England chose four different captains and 34 players during the 1988 Test Series. One senior figure was asked if this was part of a plan to prepare for the scheduled winter tour of India. He replied: 'There is no plan.' Cricket followers longed for a long-term strategy. Commentators said it was vital to gather talented players, expose them to international competition and nurture them to maturity. English cricket required leaders who would ensure this policy eventually bore fruit.

What about business? British companies can develop, providing they imitate, innovate and implement. As Alan Hodgson pointed out in an article in *Personnel Management*, they certainly have the talent. The Japanese Ministry of International Trade have studied significant inventions since the Second World War and these show that:

- 6% came from Japan;
- 14% came from France;
- 22% came from USA;
- 57% came from UK.

British managers hold the key to capitalising on this innovation. Hodgson writes:

> . . . Deming [the guru of quality management] points out that at least 85% of the failures in any organisation are the fault of systems controlled by the management. Fewer than 15% of the problems are actually worker-related. Management, and man-

agement alone, is now responsible for the transformation of western business . . . [10]

Leaders can invest in Research and Development (R & D) and educate their people about trends in the world. They must also show the benefits of change. Why? Attitude turn-around-time – thinking in another way – is often more important than technical turn-around-time. People who accept the reasons for change are more likely to respond quickly. They will use the appropriate technology and deliver the right results.

Not everybody can be a George Duncanson, Mother Teresa or Brian Clough; but many more people can know the joy of building a successful team. One way they can do this is to follow the ten steps. Chapter one has given an overview of the leader's role; the following chapters describe the other nine steps in greater detail. Leaders rely on their team members to do the job: whether they are running BA workshops, feeding the hungry in India or playing in the football league. This brings us to the next step.

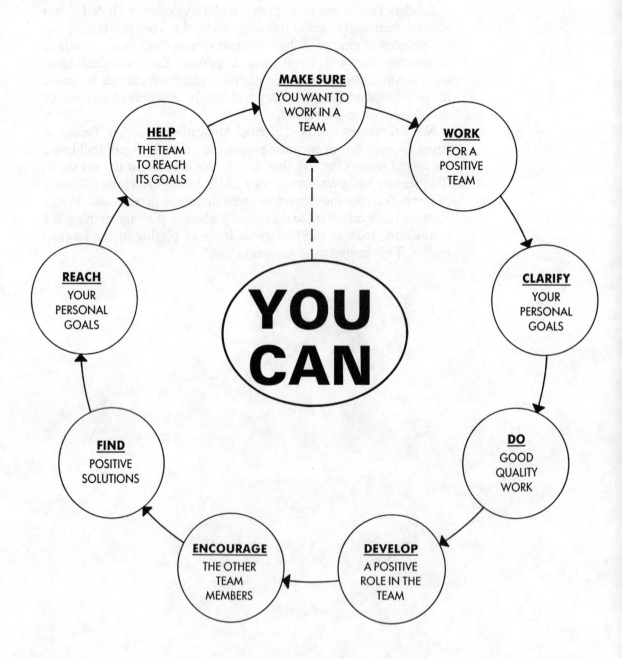

Chapter 2

HOW TO BE A POSITIVE TEAM MEMBER

When everything else is equal, the team with the best attitude will get the best results. The USA ice-hockey team, for example, beat the Soviet Union to win the 1980 Olympic Gold Medal in Lake Placid. Attitude – plus ability – led to their achievement. Sports managers look for players who play with their hearts. Why? One manager put it this way: 'Talented players can adorn a game, but they need character if they are going to change it.'

Leaders are only as good as their people. James Woodman is the managing director of Priority Services, Federal Express (UK). Speaking warmly of his truck drivers, he says: 'We have 900 ambassadors out on the road who are all self-motivating. We live our values through our people.' The firm creates 'quality heroes' by publicising 'legendary acts of service during the last month'. Federal Express attract staff who could get a job elsewhere, but who prefer to stay with them. They need people who *choose* to work for the company.

Lee Iacocca could hardly be called a 'softy' in the hard world of business. The Chrysler boss is extremely money-conscious, but even he has said: 'In the end, all business operations can be reduced to three words: people, products, and profits. People come first. Unless you've got a good team, you can't do much with the other two.'[1] People make the difference. They build the cars, drive the lorries or score the goals in ice-hockey games.

THE OLYMPIC TEAM THAT BECAME A TEAM

Derek managed an under-performing international basketball team. Their last ten matches had resulted in two victories and eight defeats. After attending a course I ran on 'sporting success', he invited me to work with him as a consultant. I sat beside him on the bench and gave my reactions after the matches. Team spirit was a problem. People were happy when the team was leading, but falling behind led to problems. Negative players complained and poisoned the air with criticism. Average players began to hide. They felt afraid of making mistakes and refused to take responsibility. Their mind-set was: 'Here we go again'. They stopped performing half-way through the game and almost welcomed losing. The players demonstrated attitudes which were similar to those found in some organisations (see illustration).

PEOPLE IN THE TEAM

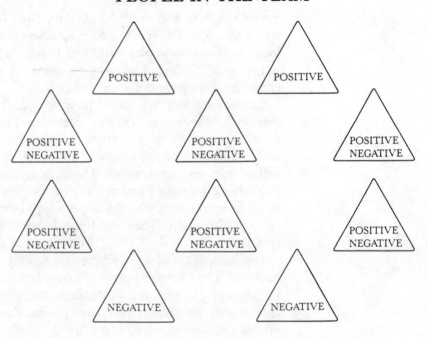

20% were super-positive

They were the team's engine. Such players supplied the enthusiasm and energy which kept everybody going. 'Come on, we can do it', was their typical cry. They played with their hearts as well as with their hands. They weren't superhuman, however, and felt isolated when other players stopped trying in matches. Derek had to give them more encouragement.

60% were both positive and negative

Sometimes they felt up; sometimes they felt down. When the team were winning, they kept their discipline and made the set-plays. When the team were losing, they fell under the influence of the negative people. They stopped following instructions, neglected the basics and began complaining. Derek realised he must get more from these 'ordinary' players if he was to improve the team.

20% were negative

Some were very talented, but they refused to take responsibility. They criticised the team's accommodation, food and training methods, before moving on to blame Derek for bad tactics. They wanted to set the rules and run the team their way, but always found excuses for their own poor performance. Two senior players said they had 'seen it all before', and expected the manager to be sacked. They felt they would survive. 'After all,' they reasoned, 'we are the best players in the country.'

Derek made a fresh start with his team. He outlined his plans to the national basketball federation and received their full backing. He then selected an inspiring captain and chose his squad for the next tournament. He picked all the positive players and several from the 'ordinary' category. Negative players were dropped and replaced by promising youngsters. Welcoming his new squad to the pre-tournament camp, he said:

> Basketball is a team game. You have been chosen because you are talented team players. Apart from being strong individuals, you follow set-plays, help colleagues who are in trouble and run until you drop. Sean, for example, is an international-class player; but he never complains, even if we replace him in the last quarter. We have two aims in this tournament: to have fun and to use it as a training ground. Why? We are preparing a team to qualify for the Olympic Games. You will stay in the troupe if you show a good attitude. We believe in positive discipline. On the court we want you to do your best and follow the team's pattern. Off the court we want you to be polite to our hosts and behave in a mature fashion. Players who disagree with these rules still have time to leave the troupe. I will meet you each individually to discuss your personal goals. We will look at this tournament and the countdown to the Olympic Games. Feel free to talk about any problems or practical ways we can

'We have 900 ambassadors out on the road who are all self-motivating. We live our values through our people'.
James Woodman, *managing director of Priority Services, Federal Express (UK).*

help you as an athlete. We will be very supportive and very demanding, but that's what you expect at international level. Training begins in 30 minutes: see you on court.

Derek's team didn't perform miracles; but they did improve their record. They won five and lost five of the next ten matches. Nothing remarkable, but they began to build a real team and expected a few setbacks. Athletes like clear messages, providing they can see the reasons, and team spirit rocketed. They now had a long-term goal: 'To qualify for the Olympics.'

'My job isn't like sports; I can't drop people', you might say. Common sense still applies. If your team is climbing a mountain, you can't have one sub-team who spend their time dragging other climbers down on to the glacier. Start by winning the 80% positive majority; they will create a winning feeling in the team. What about the 20% negative minority? They must accept the rules of teamwork, both the pluses and the minuses, otherwise they should become freelancers. If you can't win them or ignore them, help them to move on in the best possible way. The alternative is suicide for the team.

THE POSITIVE TEAM MEMBER

People want the three major things from work: money, meaning and magic. They need money to feed the stomach, meaning to feed the spirit, and magic to feed the soul. People find different ways to fulfil these needs. Some work alone; some work in a team; some become leaders. Imagine, then, that you have been asked to join a team. Here are ten steps you can follow to be a good team member. You may want to ask people to follow similar steps in your back-home working team.

1: YOU CAN MAKE SURE YOU WANT TO WORK IN A TEAM

Do you really want to be part of a team? People can take at least three roads towards doing creative work. Choosing the right road is the best way to use your talents and help other people. Let's look at each of these routes.

You can work as an individual

Sheila is a freelance consultant who conducts courses in stress management. Five years ago she left the 'security' of a regular job to set up her own firm. Now she has her office at home, travels on the road for 120 days and earns £25,000 a year. Many other people choose to work alone. These include painters, poets, plumbers, shopkeepers, window cleaners and freelance journalists. Sounds enticing, but there are two sides:

The pluses
Sheila is her own boss. She can make her own decisions and rely on her own efforts. No negotiating with troublesome colleagues or sitting in endless meetings. She can be independent, create her own work and reap the benefits.

The minuses
She must stay healthy, work hard and take responsibility for herself. Holidays are a thing of the past and market forces buffet her business. 'Selling herself' is a chore, but must be done to pay the bills. Travelling cuts into her time, but it is balanced by the days she spends at home.

Sheila accepts the whole package. The first years were difficult, but now she has found her feet. Stress management has become a popular training option in companies and she is booked for the next six months. She is even planning to take her own advice and have a holiday this year.

You can work in a team, organisation or company

Gifford Pinchot's book *Intrapreneuring* provides the most quoted example of someone who followed this road. He catalogues the story of Art Fry, the 3M employee who invented the yellow 'Post-it' note. He writes:

> . . Art began working on Post-it notes in 1974 while in church. He had been singing in a choir – two services every Sunday – and would mark the selected hymns from his hymnal with slips of paper. Although these bookmarks worked well for him during the first service, by the second service some of the paper markers would fall out. He decided he needed a marker that

> *The team member's first job is to reach his or her personal targets.*

would adhere to the page but not damage it when it was pulled off. Taking advantage of a 3M policy that gives technical people 15% of their time to work quietly on ideas of their own, Art began work on a prototype peelable hymnal marker.[2]

Pinchot says that Fry had a vision for a new class of products and created it using the tools available to him within the existing system. 3M encouraged him and this led to a win/win situation for the inventor and the company. He continues:

> As Art explains, 'Most people are really their own stumbling blocks because they don't use the freedom they have.' At first that freedom may not be much, but as an intrapreneur becomes successful, he can expect greater access to company resources.

Art Fry chose the right company in which to try his Post-it ideas, but he still had frustrations along with the triumphs. Let's look at the pluses and minuses he might find when working in an organisation.

The pluses
He enjoyed a regular pay packet, social contact and access to resources. Big is not always beautiful, but it can get things done. 3M encouraged him to use his talents, become an intrapreneur and invent his own job. He felt proud to work for a company which helped its people to be creative.

The minuses
Art worked for a go-ahead company: it's more realistic, therefore, to explore the minuses experienced by people who work for other employers. Staff sometimes feel like stokers on the Titanic. Why? The ship takes ages to turn away from the iceberg, even if the captain spots it on the horizon. Organisations confuse activity with results: staff often attend boring meetings, transfer unnecessary papers or fix details that do not matter. 'Security' is often an illusion because those on the bridge can't see where the ship is heading. Stay above the water-line and keep a life-belt. Better still: join the right ship. Art did this at 3M.

You can work as a leader

We explored this area in Chapter One so we will only look at it briefly. People become leaders for different reasons. Laura and

Bernard Ashley wanted to turn their talents into a profitable business. Steve Jobs, formerly of Apple and now of NeXT Inc, USA, got so frustrated in his former work-place that he created his own organisation. Peter Ueberroth became president of the 1984 Los Angeles Olympic Organising Committee because he was offered the chance of a lifetime. Alec Dickson is a respectable but radical Englishman who became a leader because he wanted to build a better world. He set up Voluntary Service Overseas in the early 1950s and recruited young people to work in the developing countries. 'But there was work to do in Great Britain,' he says, so he created Community Service Volunteers. Alec steered CSV until handing over to his successor in the late 1960s. Let's explore the pluses and minuses he encountered as a leader.

The pluses

He loved his work, led a motivated team and saw visible results. CSV offered young people the chance to work in, for example, mental hospitals, adventure playgrounds, nursing homes, remand centres and homes for the physically handicapped. Alec saw the volunteers develop, care for other people and contribute to society.

The minuses

He faced an ongoing fight for funds, because some establishment figures thought CSV was too radical. His first staff were devoted, but some who joined later believed the organisation was too conservative; so he had to listen to their ideological speeches. Alec saw it was impossible to please everybody and sometimes made unpopular decisions. He loved his vocation, however, and accepted the whole leadership package. The rewards outweighed the costs.

Which of the three roads do you want to follow? Explore the pros and cons of working as an individual, in an organisation or as a leader. If you choose the second road, you will eventually become part of a team. Let's take a look at the next step.

2: YOU CAN WORK FOR A POSITIVE TEAM

Look for an organisation you believe in. United Biscuits, Sainsbury and Johnson & Johnson, for example, are three of the many companies who produce written credos. Do they live their values?

Read Bob Reynolds' book *The 100 Best Companies to Work for in the UK* or study *Business* magazine's annual list of the most admired firms in Britain. Look for those that score high marks for innovation, corporate citizenship or your own particular area of interest. Talk with the company's past and present employees: they will say if the employers live up to the written credo.

Look for a mission you believe in. Katrin Adam, for example, is a German-born architect who runs a practice in New York City. Her team are committed to 'social architecture – really working with people to improve their environment.' Social projects are seldom self-supporting, however, so they also work in the private sector. They need professionals who can earn big money serving multi-national banks and supermarkets, yet who can also emphathise with low-income families on the Lower East Side. How can they attract such staff? They took one step in this direction by publicising their mission in the early 1980s.

- We want to create a structure which makes the skills of an architect available to those in most need.

- We are committed to supporting women.

- We want to promote and accommodate, in our design work and our lives, the idea of a more integrated personal work-life.

- We want to reinforce others in the pursuit of gaining control of their housing situation and environment.

- We are committed to the idea that architecture must serve people.

- We want our designs to be such that they allow for social change.

- We want to change the presently established roles and work process between architect, builder and client.[3]

Look for a leader *and* team you believe in. Peter Ueberroth, for example, is a leader who attracts good workers. He has a simple philosophy when hiring people: 'If a person had talent, the ability to grow, and loyalty – the three characteristics I've always looked for in employees – that person had a chance with me, regardless of sex, race, creed, age, or education.'[4] One key point: the leader might leave, so ensure it's a good team. Get yourself hired, even if it means working for nothing for a time. Challenging? Yes, but not as painful as suffering in a bad team.

3: YOU CAN MAKE A POSITIVE COMMITMENT TO YOUR WORK

Carole works in a comprehensive school as an English teacher. Despite government cut-backs in the past ten years, she still loves helping the students. While recognising it's hard to change the educational system, she focuses on her strengths and possibilities. Before returning to school in September, she lists what she can and can't do in her work. She finds this helps to clarify her professional goals for the academic year. Carole's two columns, for example, can read:

What I can do in my work

1   I can create a beautiful classroom.
2   I can make English lessons enjoyable and effective.
3   I can help the students to set specific goals.
4   I can help the students to pass their exams.
5   I can offer the students some of the skills they will need in the work-place.
6   I can involve the students in relevant projects.
7   I can give the students hope for the future.
8   I can make good relationships with the parents.
9   I can do my best to satisfy both the students and parents.
10 I can do my best to help the school to reach its goals.

What I can't do in my work

1   I can't change the government's education policy.
2   I can't change some of the school staff.
3   I can't give unlimited time to all the students.
4   I can't work miracles with unmotivated students.
5   I can't 'save' every student.

Carole still wants to change the educational system in order to help more students, but realises this calls for adopting a different strategy. She may have to set up an alternative school, write a best-selling book or find some other way to influence decision makers. She does not feel ready to take this step yet however, so she chooses to work inside the system at a school she believes in. Tackling this exercise helps to clarify her present possibilities. (You may also wish to do this exercise in the section below.) Carole then commits herself to doing what she can in her work as an English teacher.

MY COMMITMENT TO MY WORK

Make two lists under the following headings.

Try to think of everything you can and can't do in your work.

What I can do in my work	What I can't do in my work
1 I can	1 I can't . . . .
2 I can	2 I can't . . . .
3 I can	3 I can't . . . .
4 I can	4 I can't . . . .
5 I can	5 I can't . . . .
6 I can	Build on five things you can do and use these as a basis for
7 I can	clarifying your professional goals. You may also wish to
8 I can	do something to tackle one of the things you feel you cannot
9 I can	influence. Make a commitment to making these happen.
10 I can	

4: YOU CAN CLARIFY YOUR PERSONAL GOALS

Nordstrom run 36 speciality stores in the western part of the United States. Their employees are encouraged to take charge of their own jobs and treat their customers like gods and goddesses. Levering, Moskowitz and Katz underline this point in their book *The 100 Best Companies to Work for in America*. They ask:

> How would you like to work for a company that continually posts reminders? Reminders such as these:

> 'Make a daily 'to do' list.'
> 'What is the best use of my time now?'
> 'List goals, set priorities.'

That's the way Nordstrom is. You might have a conversation with a manager during the course of a day, and he or she might say to you, 'By the way, what are your goals for today?' If you don't like to work in a 'gung-ho' atmosphere where people are always revved up, this is not the place for you. But Nordstrom does clearly have something going for it – and it has a lot to do with those simple reminders.[5]

You don't have to go as far as Nordstrom, even though this method has contributed to their remarkable reputation for customer care. It is good to meet your boss, however, to agree on your personal aims for the next year. My players in the Swedish football team, for example, met me to make a clear working contract for the season. They wrote down their goals before the meeting and we discussed these during the session.

When I met Per, our goal-scoring centre-forward, for example, I asked him: 'What are your aims for the season?'

'I want to score 20 goals,' he replied.

We needed him to do this if we were to win trophies, but he also had to develop as a team player. I wanted him to see his part in helping the team to reach its targets.

'We have skilful forwards and good midfield players, so we will play attacking football,' I said. 'Sometimes we will be under pressure, however, and defend near our own goal. That's when we need your help. You have the ability to find space, receive the ball and shield it until our players get up the field. When we are defending, then I want you to drop back to the half-way line. Our defenders can look up, see you and pass the ball to your feet. Can you see my reasons for asking you to help us when we are defending?'

Per understood his role and suggested other ways he could help the team at throw-ins, free kicks and corners. The session lasted over an hour and he concluded by writing his personal goals.

Whether you play football, work in Nordstrom or make Post-it notes, it's useful to make a clear working contract with your boss. (Chapter Six will explore this whole area of dialogue goal setting and performance management.) Finish the session by writing them in your diary or on a poster, and displaying them in your room. One vital point: make sure you get the support you need to reach these goals.

5: YOU CAN DO GOOD QUALITY WORK

Carole takes a pride in her work as an English teacher. She does work she loves, makes learning fun and encourages the students to use their talents. Planning is the key to her success and she uses the 'What? Why? How? When?' model to organise her teaching. She also believes in getting her students to make finished products. Last year, for example, they created a positive notice-board and published their own journal. Why? Several students complained they felt depressed, hearing only bad news in the media. Carole responded by asking herself:

What do I want to help people to learn?

I want them to learn about the many good things happening in the world. I also want them to learn by using methods that help them in their future work – for example, interviewing, reporting, computing and publishing skills.

Why do I want them to learn this?

I want them to become aware of these events because it will offer them hope for the future. Learning the various skills will equip them to pass exams and prepare for work-life in the future.

How can I help them to learn this in an enjoyable and effective way?

I can ask them to find five good news stories each week by reviewing the newspapers, magazines, television and radio – for example, charity events, medical cures and indications of improved super-power relations.

I can ask them to interview 'local heroes' who have helped other people during their lives – for example, local people who took care of evacuees; blind people who raise money for those even less fortunate than themselves; firemen who risk their lives each day.

I can ask them to create a positive notice-board in our classroom. Five stories a week will produce 200 hopeful stories during the 40-week academic year.

I can ask them to produce their own journal to record these stories. The skills they will learn will include studying different media, interviewing people, writing reports, using the computer and desk-top publishing.

> *You have to invent your ideal job, you will never see it advertised.*

When do I want to begin?

I want to link this to the GCSE project work and begin next week.

Carole has a lot of knowledge to offer her students. At the same time, however, she wants them to learn how to learn and produce visible results. She achieves this balance by following a 1-2-3 model in her teaching (see illustration). The students vote with their feet.

CAROLE'S TEACHING MODEL

Begin the session.
Win and inspire people in my way.

1   Introduce the first theme.

Give people a short introduction to the theme.
Give people lots of colourful examples.
Give people positive models and examples.
Give people a practical model or tools they can use.

2   Give an activity on the theme.

Give people some learning-by-doing.
Give people a chance to 'own' the knowledge.
Give people a chance to use their energy in a positive way.
Give people a practical exercise, role-play, etc.
Give people a chance to clarify what they have learned.
Give people a chance to produce some finished product.

3   Sum up the theme.

Give people a chance to present their conclusions.
Give people another summary of the model.
Give people some idea of how they can use it in their daily lives and work.
Give people something of take-home value.
Link to the next theme.
Repeat the 1-2-3 model.
Keep going until you have finished the session.

> *Team workers need to spend 80% of their time performing excellent work and 20% encouraging their colleagues.*

Many stay after school hours to work on projects, rehearse plays or improve their writing skills. Winning the parents is another part of her job, so she sets aside time to explain to them why the students are engaged in particular projects. She performs good quality work and satisfies her customers.

6: YOU CAN DEVELOP A POSITIVE ROLE IN THE TEAM

'You have to invent your ideal job, you will never see it advertised.' Creative people follow this golden rule and the same principle applies in teamwork. Good leaders will encourage you to *express*, rather than *suppress*, your talents. Some leaders don't have time to do this, however, so you may need to educate them to use people's strengths. Start with yourself. You can take five steps to develop your own role in the team.

You can clarify your strengths

What are your talents? Per, for example, had the ability to find goal-scoring positions in the penalty area. When he hit problems, however, he lost confidence and dropped back into midfield. Per had a duty to his talents and the team: so we urged him to get back into match-winning positions. Returning to the attack gave him a greater chance to use his strengths. What do you do best? Are you good at writing, teaching, fixing machines, meeting people, or something else? Write a list of ten things you do well.

You can clarify your best way to serve the team

People have different strengths: they can serve the team in different ways. Brian Epstein recognised this when he channelled the talents of John, Paul, George and Ringo into The Beatles. The team leader's role is to ensure the necessary practical tasks get done; to give everybody a chance to be creative; to guide the team to success. Leaders do not always have time to tackle this second, creative part, so you may need to develop your own creative role. Clarify your best working style. How can you use your strengths to help the team? Do you work best by yourself, in a small team or in a larger group? Clarify how following this style will benefit the team.

You can make a clear contract with your boss and your team

Good sports coaches ensure players understand and respect the role of everybody in the team. Good leaders follow the same rule, whether they run a hotel, airline or bank. What happens if your leader fails to give everybody this kind of picture? Take the initiative by making a clear contract about your role. Show how you can use your talents and outline the rewards for the team. Make a clear working contract and agree on how to 'sell' this to the other team members. Show them how your fresh role will help the team to succeed.

You can deliver positive results

Per met his targets. He got into the penalty area, scored 25 goals and helped our defence. The last time I talked to him he had a new target: to get into the under-21 Swedish national team. Maybe he will make it, maybe not. During the time we worked together, however, he fulfilled his personal contract and helped the team to reach their goals.

Life is not always easy. Sometimes you must earn the right to develop your own role in the team. If your boss remains unconvinced about your ability to perform, work in your free time to produce the goods. You will then have more chance to use your strengths.

7: YOU CAN ENCOURAGE THE OTHER TEAM MEMBERS

Companies are now inviting their staff to develop their people skills as well as their technical skills. Why? Professionals can do even better work if they know how to support their colleagues. The old 80/20 rule provides a rough guide. Team workers need to spend 80% of their time performing excellent work and 20% encouraging their colleagues. They will then build a good climate, generate ideas and produce results.

Eric Layton, for example, was a superb team worker. He was the director of Croft House, a therapeutic community for former mental patients in East Molesey, Surrey. Like many encouragers, he had good people skills. When visitors came to the house, for instance, he knew how to get the first ten seconds right. He met them at the door, offered them a cup of tea and made them feel special. Eric always

Like Antoine de Saint-Exupéry, Eric Layton believed in looking for the 'murdered Mozart' in each person. He told the person what he saw them doing right and suggested they do it more often.

gave 100% attention to each person, whether he was helping a resident with their National Insurance or educating a trainee like myself. He was warm, caring and made people feel wanted. Eric encouraged people to use their strengths. He asked me, for example, to concentrate on working with young people. He had two reasons. First, he explained, at the age of 22, I knew their language and culture. Many came from working-class backgrounds, so I recognised their hopes, while the older residents tended to come from middle-class families. In addition, he said, as this was one of my first jobs in people-work, I needed a success. I would have the opportunity to widen my experience in later years. Eric had the same philosophy with the other team members. He invited them to do what they did well, increase their confidence and then go on to other challenges. He was an encourager rather than a stopper. A resident might have the psychiatric diagnosis of 'schizophrenic', for example, but Eric looked for the moments when he or she 'came alive'. This might be when they were gardening, fixing a motor-bike or painting a picture. Like Antoine de Saint-Exupéry, he believed in looking for the 'murdered Mozart' in each person. He told the person what he saw them doing right and suggested they do it more often. 'Would you like to do this kind of thing for a living?' was one of his favourite questions. He reinforced good experiences and helped people to blossom. He put messages in a positive way. If a person was mumbling in a meeting, for example, he would ask: 'Could you possibly speak a little louder?' A stopper, on the other hand, would have said, 'Speak up. I can't hear you.' When he saw a person doing something wrong, Eric still had the ability to give an alternative. 'I would prefer you to do it this way in the future' he said. While stating his point of view, he gave the person a chance to improve. He became a mentor for many young staff members who eventually ran their own therapeutic communities.

8: YOU CAN FIND POSITIVE SOLUTIONS TO PROBLEMS

Bill was running into difficulties. A senior manager in a car factory, he wanted his staff to take responsibility for solving problems at their own level. 'I hold meetings where I ask my blokes to talk about problems,' he said, 'but we seem unable to make headway. They simply blame the management for all their ills.' A well-meaning person, he played into the hands of the complainers who were reluctant to take initiatives. We changed the format. People were asked to attend the next meeting with solutions rather than problems. They could identify a difficulty, outline the possible solutions, and list the pluses and minuses of each option. Bill would then give a direct 'Yes' or 'No'. Some staff resisted this approach at first, but then got into the spirit. One team, for example, suggested it would be more efficient for them to talk directly with third-party customers, rather than communicate through the management chains of both companies. Bill welcomed this suggestion, even if it meant taking power from his own middle managers. His staff began to take responsibility for developing their own work practices.

Digital promote this kind of self-management. They see it as an antidote to stifling bureaucracy which can rob staff of the power to influence their own work. Win Hindle, one of DEC's top officers, says, 'People are responsible for the success of the projects they propose. He who proposes, does.' Founder Ken Olsen puts it this way: 'I believe that the worker always knows more about his job than the boss.'[6] Whichever organisation they work for, team members can help their colleagues by presenting possible solutions.

9: YOU CAN REACH YOUR PERSONAL GOALS

David Hemery reached his personal target by winning the Gold Medal in the 400-metre hurdles at the 1976 Montreal Olympics. His preparation was similar to that of many peak performers who have a clear goal. He preferred to focus on his own task, rather than worry about his opponents. He aimed to run the final in 48.4 seconds, thus beating the world record which stood at 49.11. Providing he ran his own race, and achieved this time, he stood every chance of winning the title. Apart from the physical training, Hemery prepared himself mentally. During the run up to the Games, for example, he used mental rehearsal to visualise himself winning the race. He pictured himself being drawn in lane one and then ran the race in his head. He then rehearsed competing from lanes two, three, four and so on. The next stage was to rehearse for different weather conditions, such as sunshine and rain, and different efforts from opponents. He also made his action plan for qualifying through the heats and reaching the final. Waiting for the starter's pistol in the final, Hemery relaxed in the blocks and repeated his personal affirmation: 'Today at this instant is when I have to run the best race of my life.' He took the lead, out-distanced his opponents and set a new world record of 48.1. Several days after winning the title he helped Great Britain's 400-metre relay team to win a Silver Medal. Hemery learned a great deal about himself while striving to do his best. 'If I had broken my leg the day before the Games,' he said, 'it would have been worthwhile.' He enjoyed the journey as well as the victory.

The team member's first job is to reach his or her personal targets. This calls for setting clear goals, working hard and being a good finisher. Like David Hemery, however, it may also mean going on to help the team to reach its target. This brings us to the final step.

10: YOU CAN HELP THE TEAM TO REACH ITS GOALS

Sometimes it's 'all hands on deck'. Lifeboat crews help each other to save shipwrecked sailors. Firemen help each other to rescue trapped people in burning houses. Theatre technicians and actors help each other to get things right on the opening night. Few people worry about job descriptions when they must work together to reach their targets. Part of your job is to help the team during change, challenge and crisis.

British Midland's staff, for example, showed unflagging determination when one of their aircraft crashed onto the M1 in 1989. They arranged for relatives to be picked up in taxis, flown from Ireland and, if necessary, put in touch with social workers. Michael Bishop, the chief executive, said: 'We are judged by the way we behave in these situations.' Under the glare of the spotlights, he spoke honestly and answered all the reporters' questions. It's hard to speak of 'credit' in such circumstances. British Midland, however, emerged with respect from what is sometimes called 'crisis management.' As one relative put it, 'Nothing was too much trouble.' People worked together to achieve a common goal.

Look back at these ten steps and ask yourself some hard questions:

- What do you feel about being a team worker?

- Is it the right road for you to follow?

- Can you travel along it and do creative work?

If the answer is 'No' to any of these questions, then think twice. You may spend 80% of your time doing excellent work, but fail to spend the remaining 20% encouraging other people. Take responsibility for your future. Find a new job inside the organisation, join another team or set up your own business. If the answer is 'Yes' then re-commit yourself to your work and continue to be a good team member.

Chapter 3

HOW TO BUILD A POSITIVE CULTURE

3M's culture hits you as soon as you enter their UK headquarters at Bracknell. The receptionist greets you by name and ensures you have a good place in the car park. You are then invited to walk around the exhibition which displays the company's various products, such as Post-it notes and Scotch tape, or you can read about their sponsorship of the Olympic Games. Your host arrives, offers you coffee and then it's down to business. People are friendly, optimistic and results-oriented.

Anita Roddick pays great attention to culture: the way we do things around here. She believes retail is theatre and this is reflected in small details. The Body Shop's franchises offer customers a similar experience – colours, displays and product range – whether they are located in Exeter, Heathrow or Edmonton, Canada. The company also believes in caring for the planet as well as making profits. People are buying more than a product: they are reinforcing their own values. Losing the culture could mean losing the customers.

Federal Express have flattened the pyramid and built an entrepreneurial culture. They have a central vision and decentralised responsibility. The company has a one-sentence goal which is short, simple and specific. Packages must be delivered 'Absolutely, positively on time.' Everybody, from telephonist to truck driver to top manager, can describe the goal and their part in reaching it. Staff are given 100% support to do the job. They take initiatives and are willing to be judged by their results. Federal Express stands or falls by the efforts of its people.

Frederick Smith, the company's founder, says, 'Our managers are told that their employees don't work for them, they work for their employees.' One middle manager says, 'We give people the resources to do the job and then let them loose.' Couriers are key employees and, for example, were asked to design their own uniforms. 'They

> *When in doubt, start by giving your people support. This is not only moral. People will repay you by putting their hearts into their work.*

have rewarding jobs,' said one manager. 'People are anxious to receive their packages, so delivering them is like delivering 30 birthday presents each day.' I love my job,' said one courier. 'It's like running my own business.'

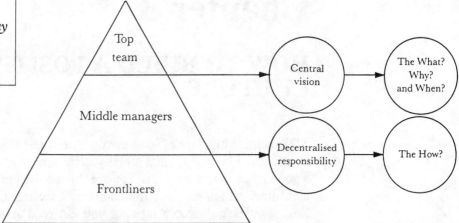

John Sculley found a huge difference in culture when he moved to Silicon Valley. Pepsi was a fine company but rather conservative. Their staff did a good job but had no mission to change the world. Apple people were different and this called for changing his leadership style. 'I largely work with people who already are motivated by the company's mission to bring the power of computing to individuals' he says in his book *Odyssey*. Describing Steve Jobs, co-founder of the company, he writes:

> He and many of Apple's leaders weren't managers at all: they were impresarios . . . It is an important metaphor for inspiring creativity. Not unlike the director of an opera company, the impresario must cleverly deal with the creative temperaments of artists.[1]

Sculley was fascinated by the constant rap sessions until he saw Apple were in financial trouble. He realised the 'impresario' must also have good business sense: otherwise the show will close and the artists will be waiting on tables. He concluded that anarchy in organisations is like arsenic: a bit is good for you, while a lot can kill you. Apple were suffering from an overdose.

How do you change a culture? David Clutterbuck and Walter Goldsmith offer four guidelines in their book *The Winning Streak*. The gist of their message is:

First: identify the culture you have.

Second: identify what kind of culture best fits the market you operate in.

Third: consider what organisational changes have to be made to accommodate any change of culture.

Fourth: consider what personnel changes must be made. The place to start is at the top. Is the current top management team willing and capable of displaying the kind of leadership by example that will convince people below of the need for change?[2]

Here are ten steps you can take to continue building a positive culture.

1: YOU CAN MEASURE YOUR PRESENT CULTURE

George Duncanson did this at British Airways engineering workshops. The survey revealed it was important to provide a clear vision, do good internal marketing and encourage people to solve problems at their own level. Discovering what people thought about the management, for example, helped him to improve the workshops.

As I mentioned in Chapter One, there are two extreme kinds of culture. 'Old organisations' are often based on 'roles and power'. They have 'tall pyramids' and strict hierarchies in which orders are passed down through many levels. People follow procedures and do what they are told. Middle managers become bureaucratic, stifle creativity and shuffle papers around the organisation. Frontliners feel neglected and blame the management. What about the customers? They are considered a necessary evil. After all, they only pay money to support the organisation.

'New organisations' are based on 'support and achievement'. The top team has a clear vision, communicates it to their people and gets their commitment. They create 'flat' pyramids and expect the staff to take initiatives. People work hard and play hard. They are energetic, enthusiastic and entrepreneurial; they also bring lots of life, laughter and colour to the building. Staff are given the support they need to produce excellent results. The customers come first because they pay everybody's wages. People enjoy working for an organisation that attracts, develops and keeps good people.

There are different instruments for measuring a culture. You can, for example, ask your people to do an exercise similar to that below and opposite. Managers have to be wary, however, of commissioning an internal survey, then denying the reality of feedback. 'It's not really like that,' said one company manager. 'The questionnaire was issued at a bad time during the pay negotiations.' Accept your staff's suggestions; then follow up the survey by making visible improvements.

MEASURING THE CULTURE

You can ask your people to grade – on a scale from 0 to 10, where 0 is low and 10 is high – where they think your organisation stands at the present time in each of the following areas. They can do their part by being honest. You can do your part by accepting it as a true guide to their gut feeling and perception. The next step will be to use the information to improve the culture.

The scores are a guide. Whether people give 0 or 10, ask them to suggest practical ways the organisation can improve in each area. Implement the ideas wherever possible. Run a similar survey in six months' time and continue to improve the culture.

Poor leadership   Good leadership

0   1   2   3   4   5   6   7   8   9   10

Poor communication of the vision   Good communication of the vision

0   1   2   3   4   5   6   7   8   9   10

Poor people-management   Good people-management

0   1   2   3   4   5   6   7   8   9   10

Poor working conditions   Good working conditions

0   1   2   3   4   5   6   7   8   9   10

Poor staff commitment   Good staff commitment

0   1   2   3   4   5   6   7   8   9   10

Poor at using the staff's talents and knowledge   Good at using the staff's talents and knowledge

0   1   2   3   4   5   6   7   8   9   10

Poor quality work   Good quality work

0   1   2   3   4   5   6   7   8   9   10

Poor customer service   Good customer service

0   1   2   3   4   5   6   7   8   9   10

Poor future prospects   Good future prospects

0   1   2   3   4   5   6   7   8   9   10

Poor public reputation   Good public reputation

0   1   2   3   4   5   6   7   8   9   10

You can also ask people to give their views on the following areas:

The organisation's strengths are:

1 . . . .

2 . . . .

3 . . . .

The organisation's weaknesses are:

1 . . . .

2 . . . .

3 . . . .

The organisation can be improved by:

1 . . . .

2 . . . .

3 . . . .

2: YOU CAN DECIDE TO BUILD A POSITIVE CULTURE

IBM, for example, have built a culture based on certain values which are expressed in their vision. People feel inspired to reach the goal and this leads to increased vitality. They work hard and achieve visible results. This in turn reinforces their values. Whatever kind of culture you decide to build, try to make sure that you have the right relationship between values and results:

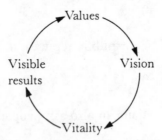

Healthy cultures are, I believe, based on the three Es: encouragement, enterprise and excellence. Encouragement is the first building block. Why? People need practical support if they are to have the strength for anything beyond survival. Otherwise some will succeed, while others will become cynical. The next building block is to provide incentives for becoming entrepreneurial. In this sort of culture, people will enjoy the rewards and do their best to achieve excellence. Leaders who offer these things will reap the benefits. They will build a company – or a society – where everybody can be winners.

Let me give my personal opinion of how one company, IBM, rates in each of these areas.

● Encouragement

IBM get high marks in this respect. They take care of their staff, train managers to be good encouragers and make people feel ten feet tall. They show it is profitable to support their own staff in the hard world of business. My subjective view is to give them 8 out of 10.

● Enterprise

Despite massive profits, IBM people give their own company a mixed rating. Some departments, such as marketing, get a 9 or 10: other departments, such as administration, get a 2 or 3. Size is a problem. It's hard to listen to your customers if you are protected by layers of padding. Staff thought they were selling: but they were simply taking orders. John Akers, their chief executive, has changed the mood of self-congratulation which led to profits plunging in the mid-1980s. People are being asked to become more entrepreneurial and to take greater initiatives in their work.

- Excellence

IBM prides itself in exceeding expectations and their surveys reveal over 97% customer satisfaction. This sounds great, but, as IBM itself has pointed out, the sheer volume of business done by the company means that 3% adds up to many hundreds of dissatisfied customers. Customers agree the machines are good, but sometimes complain the company loses interest after clinching the sale. 'I never know who to contact,' said one customer. 'I build a relationship with one IBMer, but the next time I phone they have been moved to another department. We have to start all over again.' I would give the company 7 out of 10 for excellence.

How do you rate your own organisation in the areas of encouragement, enterprise and excellence? How do you rate British Rail? How do you rate the present government in their way of running Britain? When in doubt, start by giving your people support. This is not only moral. People will repay you by putting their hearts into their work.

3: YOU CAN MAKE PLANS FOR CHANGING THE CULTURE

Watford Football Club were languishing in Division Four when Elton John became their chairman in 1977. He began by creating a

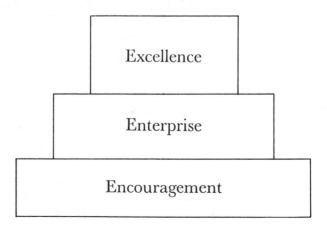

clear vision: they aimed to become 'the family football club.' The next step was to build a good top team. He invited Graham Taylor to be manager and hired several high class administrators. The third step was to change the club's image. He altered the team's colours from black and amber to red and gold. While retaining elements of tradition, this provided an attractive image which appealed to a family audience. The fans were impressed, but they wanted more visible success. Watford won promotion from Divisions Four, Three and Two. They played attacking football and rose to the top half of Division One. They refurbished the stadium, removed the greyhound track which surrounded the playing pitch, and reached the Cup Final at Wembley. The club suffered a setback in 1987, however, when Elton John appeared to lose interest and they lost Graham Taylor. The club fell into Division Two, but retained the public's goodwill by being the family football club.

How do you change a culture? Real change has to happen on a philosophical level. People have to think differently and eventually behave in a different fashion. As a leader, you can start by clarifying your philosophy and developing a positive vision. This takes time, however, and you may want an early success. The first step may be to change the physical things. Why? It's relatively easy to make the entrance hall attractive, create a new logo or give staff money to improve their back-home work-place. People see something is happening, but still remain suspicious. The second step is to change the psychological things: create a winning feeling by achieving some early visible success. The third step is to change the philosophical things. People will then alter the way they do things in the team, organisation or company.

4: YOU CAN CHANGE THE PHYSICAL THINGS

Winston Churchill once said, 'We shape our buildings and afterwards our buildings shape us.' In their book *The Vital Difference*, Fredrick Harmon and Garry Jacobs describe how one company reacted after leaving their original San Francisco home in 1973.

Levi Strauss moved from a 'warm, cosy, four-storey building' to a modern high rise. Staff were no longer meeting in the halls and this created divisions. Most employees worked on the lower floors but the executives had their own lift service to the 28th floor. People also complained about 'the cold, isolated feeling of working in their glass-enclosed cubicles.' Morale and productivity suffered and, even though the lease had another 13 years to run, the company res-

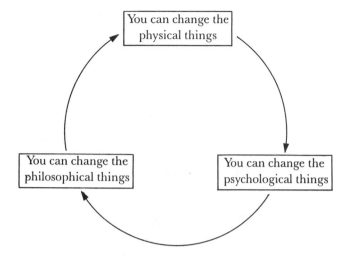

You can begin anywhere in the circle, but let's look at the easiest step first.

ponded immediately. They built their own headquarters on a site overlooking San Francisco Bay.

> When you enter Levi Strauss' offices, you have the feeling you are really in a home. On every floor there are three or four very large open-area lounges with cushioned chairs, couches, and kitchenettes, which cover a total area of about 5,000 square feet. In addition, there are dozens of open-air balconies, a 7,000-square-foot health club and a park. One woman, who was sitting on the lawn eating her lunch, summed up the attitude of employees towards the new offices: 'This is mine.'[3]

The success of the San Francisco building has led Levi Strauss to improve their 50 factories around the country. The pay-off was in the bottom-line. They got a building that was 10% more efficient in usable office space and led to higher productivity. There is lower employee turnover, a long waiting-list of people who want to work for the company and improved morale. 'But we can't move to another building' you may say. Maybe not; but you can make the work-place more user-friendly. Before making changes, however, listen to your people. *Involvement* is vital. Study the survey, follow up suggestions and involve the staff in improving their environment. Corporate changes, such as presenting a new public image, can be made at the same time. There are several benefits to making physical changes.

You can create a corporate identity

Prudential, Rowntree and ICI have all updated their public images. 'Corporate identity programmes' play a big part in helping a company to stand out from the crowd. They often involve re-designing the corporate colours, logo, uniforms, brochures, advert-isements and even buildings. Maybe you haven't the money to go to such expensive lengths: but you can put up a team photograph, display the team's goals or make a poster which shows the team's role in the company.

You can create a feeling of involvement

Canon, Toshiba and Nissan proudly declare their staff make several thousand suggestions each year and over 80% are adopted. Many ideas involve simple physical changes to make the job easier or more effective. This cannot be dismissed as a foreign phenomenon. British people want to feel involved in their work, but have seldom been given the chance. Find ways to involve your staff and both they and the company will benefit.

You can create good quality work

Model the quality you want people to produce in their work for the company. If you plan to publish a newsletter, for example, make it excellent. Make it interesting, readable and well-designed. Why? The physical changes you make will act as a tone-setter. Actions speak louder than words. It is bad modelling to talk about quality if the car park is messy or the entrance hall is depressing. Get the physical things right and people will believe you.

5: YOU CAN CHANGE THE PSYCHOLOGICAL THINGS

Swedish schools tend to be grey and dispiriting. Teachers at one school in Örebro, however, introduced some excitement after the summer holidays. When the students arrived in August, they began the term by 'celebrating the start of school'. Children arrived to find the school flag flying, a band playing in the playground and the restaurant serving special food. Teachers and students spent the next two days making the school look beautiful. This provided a good start to the academic year.

How can you build a winning feeling? Here are some suggestions:

You can have a kick-off meeting to start the working year

September 1 is a good date. Meet in a special place such as at a conference centre, on a boat or combine the meeting with a visit to the theatre. The manager's job is to welcome people, share the team's goals and show the rewards of achieving the targets. These 'happenings' can be a useful morale-booster, but they must be followed up properly, otherwise people become cynical.

You can achieve an early visible success

After taking over the Swedish football team, I set up a pre-season tournament which involved eight clubs. The first and second teams in each group of four qualified for the semi-final and an automatic bronze medal. The team I took over hadn't won anything for five years, so I organised the tournament so we played in the weakest group and were certain to qualify. The players got their hands on a medal and went from strength to strength. Apart from boosting the team's morale, this success provided the credibility I needed to attract new players and make the necessary changes.

You can encourage the positive people

Encourage the encouragers. They are your allies so give them responsibility and status. You will then protect the culture by showing, 'This is the behaviour we reward around here.' I can't underline this message enough. Managers invite failure if they spend too little time caring for the encouragers and too much time negotiating with the stoppers.

You can introduce more fun into the organisation

The newly appointed boss of an hotel chain was so struck by the lack of humour in the company that he decided to do something radical. One day he arrived at work dressed as Winnie the Pooh. The

Managers are the culture carriers who translate all the beautiful words into action.

receptionist was so taken aback that she began dialling the security guard. Eventually people got the message. While maintaining quality standards in the hotels, they began to introduce more personal service, local colour and, dare I say it, spontaneous laughter.

You can record your successes

One supermarket manager, for example, gathered his staff together on the last Friday of each month. Each department made posters headed 'Five positive things that have happened in the last month' and presented these to the whole team. He then described the whole store's achievements and looked forward to the next month. This helped to build people's confidence.

6: YOU CAN CHANGE THE PHILOSOPHICAL THINGS

Mikhail Gorbachev invited the Soviet citizens to think in a different way. 'How do you get people to take initiatives', he was quoted as saying, 'when they don't know the meaning of the word?' Gorbachev was faced by an enormous task. He had to convince, change or oust the party bureaucrats who controlled local activities. The alternative was to bypass them and go directly to the people. Gorbachev could only convince the people, however, by providing bread today, rather than jam tomorrow. Changing the physical things will lead to changing the psychological things which will change the philosophical things. People would then begin to believe in perestroika.

The values clarification model of learning underlines this message. Sidney Simon, one of its originators, says that people learn on three different levels: facts, concepts and values (see illustration). Real change has to start on the deepest level. People can argue about nuclear power, for example, by exchanging facts about output, safety records and cost. They can then discuss the concept of this kind of energy, whether or not it is environmentally friendly and should be part of our future. Positions seldom change, however, until something like Chernobyl hits people on the values level. Expert assurances mean little when the Geiger counter measures high radiation. People quickly change their values.

Transformational leaders reach people on the values level. They introduce a new paradigm, inspire people to think in a different way and deliver visible results. Martin Luther King did this with Civil

Rights in America. Anita Roddick has done it at the Body Shop. John Sculley introduced a more business-like approach at Apple. Sir John Harvey-Jones did it at ICI. How do such leaders do it? They change the physical things to change the psychological things to change the philosophical things. This is necessary to achieve lasting change.

REAL CHANGE STARTS ON THE DEEPEST LEVEL

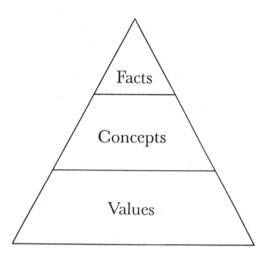

7: YOU CAN EDUCATE YOUR MIDDLE MANAGERS

John Naisbitt and Patricia Aburdene believe 'the big challenge of the 1980s is not the retraining of workers, but the retraining of managers.'[4] Middle managers are the key people in translating philosophy into action. Companies have responded to this challenge by setting up their own management academies. Why? Managers sometimes need to develop a different way of leading their people.

The old-style manager, for example, based his management style on the extremes of: 'Tell 'em and leave 'em.'

'Tell them what the problem is, tell them how to fix it and tell them when you will be back. Leave them to get on with it: then return in two hours to tell them what they have done wrong.'

Responding to calls to involve his staff more, this kind of manager said:

> *Kaizen calls for doing your best, then trying to do better than your best.*

'They just don't know how. I leave them to do jobs where they have to take initiatives, but they have no ideas. It's left to me to go in and kick them into action. I know my men. These guys are used to being told what to do. That's the way they like it. If you leave them alone they haven't got a clue. I am paid to get results – and this is the best way to do it.'

The new-style manager sounds similar but adds a middle step: 'Tell 'em, educate and involve 'em, then leave 'em.'

'Tell them about the company's goals. Educate and involve them in doing their part to reach the goals. Leave them to use their knowledge to reach their goals. Return to compliment them on their success and, if necessary, inspire them to do even better. Tell them how they have contributed to reaching the company's goals.'

This calls for a fine balance between hands-on and hands-off management. A great deal depends on company culture and there isn't any universal rule book. Hence the growth of management academies in British Airways, Digital and other companies. Managers are the culture carriers who translate all the beautiful words into action. They are the people who can shape the future culture.

8: YOU CAN CREATE A REAL INVOLVEMENT PROGRAMME

Danish Shell ran this kind of programme when re-introducing the concept of customer service. Garage owners, pump attendants and managers were asked to suggest ways the company could gain a competitive edge over their rivals. Thousands of ideas, from offering the customer a cup of coffee to redesigning the forecourts, were put forward. Many were implemented and led to an increase in market share.

Involvement programmes must be properly orchestrated. People have often attended courses, for example, where they have brainstormed ideas for improving performance, presented them on a poster and then seen nothing happen. But there is profit in these ideas. How can you set up a systematic involvement programme?

It's important:

- to explain the company's vision to people;

- to explain the areas they can influence;

- to set up a mechanism for using people's involvement, initiatives and ideas, for example, to set up an implementation team;

- to make sure managers know how to involve people;

- to make priorities concerning the areas for involvement;

- to develop a feeling of ownership;

- to use the different involvement mechanisms, such as a complete 'listening downwards' programme, giving local autonomy, practical problem-solving groups, etc.;

- to implement people's ideas for improving quality management, customer service and the organisation;

- to show visible results and publicise success stories;

- to keep your hands on the programme to make sure it improves the company's performance.

People have a great deal of talent which can be used to improve the company. But this has to be tapped in a way that fits the culture, rather than imposed from outside. When this is done correctly, involvement programmes can lead to greater job satisfaction. They can also improve the company's performance.

9: YOU CAN INTRODUCE 'KAIZEN' INTO THE ORGANISATION

'Kaizen' means 'constant improvement' and is the idea I personally like best in Japanese management. People may, for example, put the spotlight on incoming telephone calls. Staff focus on how to improve the service and implement the ideas. So far it sounds like quality circles and indeed they are simply an expression of Kaizen. After tackling other areas for improvement, people return to the incoming telephone calls to explore how to improve the improved service.

Peak performers are committed to Kaizen. Jack Nicklaus, for example, was the greatest golfer of his generation. He won more major championships than any other competitor, but Sunday's success was followed by returning to basics on Monday morning. Nicklaus strove to improve his driving, chipping and putting. Some people say this approach leads to becoming a perfectionist and excludes all enjoyment. Kaizen calls for doing your best, then trying to do better than your best. Peak performers argue it is this journey which provides all the enjoyment.

10: YOU CAN CONTINUE TO BUILD A POSITIVE CULTURE

British Rail, for example, can commit itself to building a positive culture. Why not? Danish Railways encouraged their staff to be entrepreneurial and achieved excellent results. The first step would be to commission an internal survey. Let's imagine BR's staff awarded the company 6 out of 10 when it came to using their people's talents. Many dedicated workers want to help the company: so how can the managers boost this figure to a 7, 8, 9 or 10? British Rail can ask their staff how the company can make better use of their knowledge. The next step is to implement their suggestions. One outcome might be to create an involvement programme. The staff teams at each station, for example, can find ways to give better service to their passengers. Staff know literally hundreds of ways to improve their work-place. The next step, therefore, is to find ways to improve their work practices. This does not tackle the basic issue of running an efficient rail service, but giving people freedom to use their ideas will boost their morale. Danish Railways did this and found that everybody benefited: the workers, the customers and the company. Six months after the initial survey, British Rail can re-check the rating for using their staff's talents. Kaizen then comes into the picture. Whatever the figure – be it 6, 8 or 10 – they must also ask how the company can make *even better* use of their knowledge. Why should BR use the new ideas? Apart from being a matter of survival, it is one way to keep their best people. They will show that they care for their people, products and profits. British Rail will show they want to continue to build a creative culture.

Chapter 4

HOW TO SET A POSITIVE GOAL

Francis Crick and James Watson had a mission; they wanted to discover the secret of life. Spurred on by the parallel research done by Rosalind Franklin, Raymond Gosling and Maurice Wilkins at King's College, London, they laboured day and night in Cambridge. Science might be based on co-operation, but they wanted to be the first to create a model for the DNA. One disastrous attempt was followed by their uncovering the double helix in 1953. Crick and Watson knew they had reached the target, even before re-checking the results. Why? The model looked so 'beautiful'. People will work like hell to reach a specific goal.

People like to know their part in reaching the goal. Liverpool FC's directors, for example, have said: 'The Board's job is to look ahead to the next year. The manager's job is to look ahead to the next match. The player's job is to look ahead to the next kick.' The club aims to field the best football team in England. They must sign good players, attract 35,000 spectators to each home match, make a profit, employ effective tactics and win the League Championship. Directors, administrators, coaches, players and turnstile operators know their part in helping the club to reach its target.

People like to feel they are on the right mission. 'We want to be number one,' is often quoted as a goal, but it is often unrealistic and unspecific. Wigan Rugby League Club's chairman, for example, provided a clear vision for his club. He said, 'We want to see 15,000 happy faces here every fortnight.' Their strategy was to create a better stadium, attract a family audience and play entertaining rugby. Wigan also happened to win lots of trophies; this contributed to them reaching their target.

Travel Company B wanted to ensure they were embarking on the right mission. The Managing Director wrote to me outlining his plans for a vision creation workshop in 1987. 'After two days,' he said, 'we must be sure that:

- we know which mountain we are climbing;

- we know why we are climbing it;

- we know our strategy for climbing the mountain;

- we know how to inspire our people to climb it;

- we know when we will reach the summit.'

Travel Company B began by asking themselves fundamental questions.

- what's special about us?

- what is our uniqueness?

- what business are we really in?

- what are our strengths, weaknesses, opportunities and threats?

- who are our customers?

- what do our customers want?

The second step was to clarify the goal. Where did Travel Company B want to be in 1990? What would be happening in the world? Who would be our competitors? What would be the rewards of reaching the goal?

The third step was strategy. Travel Company B had chosen their mountain:

- how could they climb it?

- what was the best way to reach the summit?

- how could they inspire their own people?

The fourth step was evaluation:

- how would they know when they had reached their goal?

- what were the behavioural checks?

The top team used the vision creation workshop to define their goal, create a strategy and make an action plan. The next step was implementation.

John Sculley describes how Apple Computers clarify their vision in *Odyssey*.

We project ourselves out into the future and then work backward to the present in small increments of time. We ask

People need to have a vision, otherwise there is a vacuum.

ourselves: what will the year 1992 be like? We create in our minds a visual portrait of what the economy, our industry and our company will look like. Then we move back into the present, envisioning what we have to do in small steps to get to the future. What do we have to do in 1989, for example, to achieve our vision in 1992? We call this 'back to the future' planning.[1]

Vision, mission, or goal: whatever you call it, having a target can stimulate people to greater efforts. Roger Bannister had a clear aim in 1953: he wanted to beat the four-minute mile. Spurred on by John Landy's challenge, he co-operated with Chris Chataway and Chris Brasher to clock 3.59.4 minutes on a rainy day in Oxford. Bannister's quest illustrated many of the qualities that contribute to having a clear vision (see below). His target was simple, specific and measurable. Reaching the goal would also be rewarding.

Peak performers tend to be obsessive. They do things because they *need* to do them, not because they want to do them. Bob Geldof, for example, was so stirred by pictures of starving children in Ethopia that he immediately began working on Band Aid. He aimed to feed the world and nothing seemed impossible. As Mother Teresa said to him later:

'There's something you can do that I can't do and there's something I can do that you can't do. The only thing is that we both have to do it.'

Geldof led from the front, inspired people to work together and achieved some of his goals. Like many leaders, however, he faced the next dilemma. What to do after Band Aid? People need to have a vision, otherwise there is a vacuum.

YOUR VISION

A vision needs to be inspiring and to have a strong impact. Here are some qualities you might like to include in your vision:

- You can make it a one-sentence goal.

- You can make it short, simple and specific.

- You can make it relevant, reachable and rewarding.

- You can make it measurable.

- You can make it visual so that people can 'see' the goal.

Here are ten things you can do to set a positive goal.

Build on your uniqueness. Be who you are, only more so.

1: YOU CAN CLARIFY YOUR STRENGTHS AND WEAKNESSES

Build on your uniqueness. Be who you are, only more so. 'Do what you do best,' is a good motto in sport, art or business. The Beatles, for example, were gifted song-writers and exciting performers. It would have been ridiculous for them to stop composing and become marathon runners. Ask yourself: 'What is special about us? What do we offer that nobody else does? What business are we in?'

Clarks Shoes are a company who believe in sticking to their last, a characteristic highlighted by David Clutterbuck and Walter Goldsmith in their book *The Winning Streak*:

> 'Every time we've diversified it has been a disaster,' says one of the company's senior managers. 'We stay in shoes,' adds Daniel Clark firmly.
>
> 'Clarks' says Daniel Clark, 'is all about brands. The company puts tremendous effort into developing and maintaining the Clarks' name. So much so that one firm of consultants, advising the company on diversification, claimed that they could put the name Clark to almost anything and it would sell. 'We have to maintain the integrity of our brands,' says Clark. 'We want them to be there in 50 years' time.' Research has shown Clarks' brand to be a remarkable seven times stronger than its nearest competitors.'[2]

Don't ignore your weaknesses. The Beatles were bad financial managers and cash problems fuelled their internal squabbles. Brian Epstein handled the money while he was alive, but his death started a financial war and led to a painful divorce. What are your weaknesses? How can you compensate for them? Do what is necessary, but don't concentrate on your weak points to the detriment of your talents.

2: YOU CAN CLARIFY YOUR OPPORTUNITIES AND THREATS

Beware of the Titanic syndrome: looking inwards, believing in your own invincibility and not noticing the icebergs. IBM and some of our trade unions have suffered from this disease. Build on your uniqueness, but see what is happening in the world.

BBC Television, for example, has many opportunities. The corporation makes high-quality programmes, sells them at a profit, employs hundreds of creative people and, with the advent of satellites, has a huge potential market. Dangers loom on the horizon, however, and must be tackled. The challenges include government pressure, licence fee worries, satellite television, internal bureaucracy and difficulty in attracting talented staff.

Look at your own working team. List their strengths, weaknesses, opportunities and threats. Clarify what they do well and what they can improve; clarify how they can capitalise on their opportunities and deal with the dangers. You will then be standing on firm ground before taking the next step.

MY TEAM'S SWOT

You can take a look at your team and the challenges they face by doing a SWOT analysis. Try to list your team's:

Strengths   Weaknesses

•   •

•   •

•   •

Opportunities   Threats

•   •

•   •

•   •

3: YOU CAN CLARIFY YOUR TARGET GROUP

Theodore Levitt, the marketing guru, has said: 'If you're not thinking segments, you're not thinking.' Who are your customers? Today it's even more vital to reach the right customers with the right product in the right way at the right price. Finding the right niche is more likely to produce the right results. James Pilditch underlines this in his book *Winning Ways*:

There are three golden rules: know your customer, give her what she wants, and give good service.

The notion of mass marketing is dwindling. It is being challenged by targeted, 'segmented' marketing made possible by flexible manufacturing . . . More and more, winning companies are those that identify and cater for this spectrum of individual tastes and preferences . . . It comes back to finding out what the customer wants more rapidly and precisely than your competitors do – then providing it.[3]

British football clubs, for example, must define their target group. Do they aim to attract families, well-behaved people or hooligans? If they aim for the first two groups, they need to provide user-friendly stadiums and attractive football. If they aim for the hooligans, they

MY TEAM'S CUSTOMERS

You can define your target groups by making a list of your team's customers and what each of these groups wants:

My team's customers

-
-
-
-

What they want

-
-
-
-
-
-
-
-
-
-

need to provide boring matches, beer and barbed wire! Who is your target group?

4: YOU CAN CLARIFY WHAT THEY WANT

Brian Walsh, chief executive for the House of Fraser, has said:

> There are three golden rules: know your customer, give her what she wants, and give good service. There are plenty more of course, normal business rules, like knowing when to mark down merchandise that isn't selling, but you must have those three rules.[4]

Look at your own team. List the team's customers and what each group wants. You will then be in a better position to define your goals.

Imagine you are a school headteacher. The first step is to list all your customers: the students, parents, potential employers and politicians. The second step is to ask each target group what they want from the school. The third step is to integrate this with what the school team wants to offer, agree on standards and set clear goals. (You may have to 'educate' some of the customers to see what school-leavers will need in the future.) The fourth step is to do good quality work and achieve customer satisfaction.

5: YOU CAN CLARIFY YOUR VISION

Visionaries are dreamers who deliver. Keep your integrity, but be realistic; feed your soul, but make sure you succeed. Remember the answers to the previous four steps: what do you want to offer people? Build on your strengths, but integrate these with your customers' desires. Create a win/win goal which benefits you, your team and your customers. The following pages offer exercises you can use to create your vision for your team.

Mary Andrews, for example, ran the computer team in a national chain of copyshops and printers. Desktop publishing was becoming cheaper and hitting the company's shops in the High Street. They were feeling the pinch and under pressure to provide better quality service to their customers. Top management decided to update the system and, after testing various models, opted for the Apple Macintosh. January was nearing its end, but they still wanted everything in place by 1 May. Mary was invited to choose ten people who would introduce the system throughout the country. She consulted her bosses and colleagues, then asked herself: 'What is the result we want to achieve?' The priority was simple: 'We want 100 people to be able to use the Macintosh by 1 May.' She then added two other main goals and broke each of them down into specific sub-goals. After brainstorming possible one-liners, Mary produced her first page under the heading of 'My vision for my team' (see below).

MAYDAY IS MACDAY

'We want . . . '

1: To train 100 people to use the Macintosh system by 1 May

a) To make sure at least three people in each branch can use the Macintosh
b) To make sure they can use word-processing, graphics and the network system
c) To equip them to train other people if necessary

2: To make sure they are good ambassadors for the Macintosh

a) To make sure they enjoy learning the Macintosh
b) To make sure they are enthusiastic about the system
c) To make sure they are able to 'sell' the pluses to other people

3: To enjoy our work as trainers and build a good training team

a) To get the support we need to do the job
b) To clarify the team's goal and strategy for helping the students to succeed. To have a structure which is student-friendly. To be able to step in for each other when necessary. To continue to be able to use our individual strengths as team members
c) To have regular meetings where we can clarify our goals, results and areas for improvement

6: YOU CAN CLARIFY THE REWARDS

People want money and meaning from their work. Akio Morita, Sony CEO, has said:

> Sometimes a sense of mission, a sense of participation and a sense of achievement are great joys. A scientist or an engineer is like an artist completely caught up in playing the piano or creating a sculpture . . . he likes his job so much that he forgets about everything else.[5]

Mary had to show her people the benefits of introducing the Macintosh system by 1 May. She began by listing the pluses for herself, the team members, the company and the customer. Under two of these headings, for example, she wrote:

Rewards for the team members

- Increased job satisfaction
- Increased knowledge
- Increased status
- More pay
- More marketability within the company

Rewards for the company

- More motivated staff who can respond to the customer's needs
- Better quality work
- Increased customer satisfaction
- More repeat custom
- Increased reputation and profits

Look at your own team's goal: why should people want to climb this particular mountain? List the rewards for each group and communicate these to your people. Apart from offering them a sense of mission, it is more likely to motivate them to want to achieve the target.

Visionaries are dreamers who deliver. Keep your integrity, but be realistic; feed your soul, but make sure you succeed.

7: YOU CAN CLARIFY THE SUPPORT YOU NEED

Woodward and Bernstein gained fame by uncovering the Watergate scandal which led to Richard Nixon's downfall in 1973. Katharine Graham, the owner of the *Washington Post*, and Ben Bradlee, the editor, deserve just as much credit. They supported their staff when the White House turned up the heat. At one point it appeared that John Mitchell, H R Haldeman and John Ehrlichman were right, while the two young journalists were wrong. Woodward and Bernstein eventually reached their goal, but they could not have done it without encouragement from their employers. Graham and Bradlee gave them the help they needed to do the job.

Mary also needed support. She brainstormed the practical help she needed in order to get people using the Macintosh system by 1 May. Her list read:

I would like

- Total support from the top
- A good attitude from my team
- People prepared to work long hours
- All the Macintosh hardware and software I need
- Staff who want to learn the system
- Other financial and practical support

List the practical help you need to be able to do your job. Check with your bosses, colleagues and staff if they are prepared to give this support. Providing they are willing to give it, you can go on to the next step.

8: YOU CAN CLARIFY THE MEASURES

Ask yourself: 'What will be happening that will tell us we have reached the goal? What will the customers be saying? What will the staff be feeling, saying, doing? What will be the visible signs?' List the behavioural checks. Mary's list, for example, read almost like a repetition of the vision.

- We will have 100 people – including three in every branch – who will be able to use the Macintosh.

- We will have 100 people who say they enjoy learning the Macintosh and who can train other people to learn it.

- We will have one team leader and ten team members who say they have enjoyed working in the team and on the project.

- We will have senior managers who tell us: 'Well done. You reached the goals and the company has benefited.'

I invite you to describe your goal, mission or vision for your team in the attached exercise. Then move on to the next stage.

My vision for my team

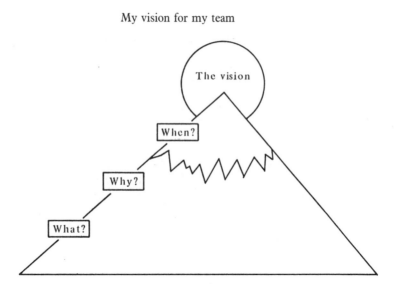

THE VISION

You can create a one-sentence goal, target or slogan.

. . . .

Now write down your main goals.

We want:

1 . . . .

Sub goals

a) . . . .

b) . . . .

c) . . . .

2 . . . .

a) . . . .

b) . . . .

c) . . . .

3 . . . .

a) . . . .

b) . . . .

c) . . . .

'Sometimes a sense of mission, a sense of participation and a sense of achievement are great joys. A scientist or an engineer is like an artist completely caught up in playing the piano or creating a sculpture . . . he likes his job so much that he forgets about everything else.' Akio Morita, *Sony CEO.*

THE REWARDS
of reaching the goals will be:

For myself

-
-
-

For the department

-
-
-

For the customer

-
-
-

For the team

-
-
-

For the company

-
-
-

For other groups

-
-
-

THE SUPPORT

we would like in order to be able to reach the goals:

1. . . . .

2. . . . .

3. . . . .

4. . . . .

5. . . . .

THE MEASURES

We will know we have reached the goals when the following things are happening:

1. . . . .

2. . . . .

3. . . . .

4. . . . .

5. . . . .

- Make these behavioural checks.

- List the physical things that will be happening that will tell you that you have reached your goals.

9: YOU CAN CLARIFY YOUR STRATEGY

Vision creation is deciding what mountain you want to climb; strategy is deciding how you want to climb it. The High Street printers' top team, for example, had agreed on the vision for the company: their 'What? Why? and When?' The next step was to work out the business strategy: their 'How?' Choosing to deliver good quality at low cost had led them to the Macintosh system.

Mary's team had followed a similar process when implementing this decision. After defining the team's goal, they now had to clarify their 'How?' Strategic thinking can be broken down into two parts:

- People need to choose an effective strategy. Choose one that will help people to feel good and get good results. The top team had opted for offering quality printing at low cost as their competitive edge. Mary believed in creating user-friendly learning systems for the students and building a positive team.

- People need to understand the reasons for choosing the strategy.

The top team needed to ensure the branch staff understood why the company was opting for quality at low cost. After all, they were the people who were going to implement it on a daily basis. Mary's team needed to understand why it was important to make the training fun, user-friendly and effective. People who see the reasons for a particular strategy are more likely to make it happen.

How do you want to climb your mountain? Should you put the emphasis on quality management, customer service, perestroika or a combination of these things? What will be effective? What will achieve the best results?

10: YOU CAN CLARIFY YOUR ACTION PLAN

Mary felt it was time to get the show on the road. Her action plan read:

- Meet my team to present the vision, get their ideas and agree on a final vision.

- Check with my bosses about the support we need.

- Delegate responsibility for arranging the Macintosh hardware, software and other equipment.

- Delegate responsibility for fixing the training centre, course dates, contacts with the branches, attractive invitations and course follow-up.

- Delegate responsibility for organising the course format.

- Spend one hour with each tutor to set personal goals and make sure they get the support they need.

- Keep an overview of the project and do everything necessary to make it succeed.

How can you get things moving in your team? You will need to clarify your goal, get commitment from your people and give them the support they need to do the job. You will also need to keep your hands on the business – yet give people freedom to be creative – and guide the team to success. It's time to make an action plan for the next week, month, six months, year and three years. Let's look at the next step.

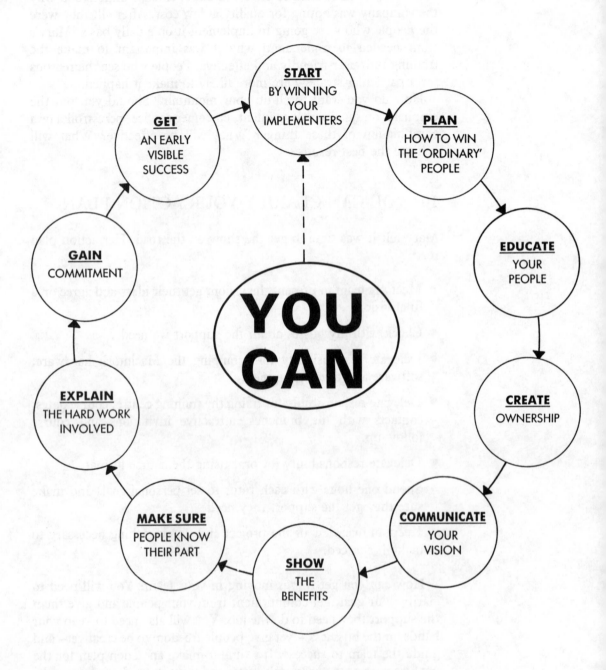

Chapter 5

HOW TO GET COMMITMENT TO REACHING A POSITIVE GOAL

Frederick Smith, founder of Federal Express, believes in winning the hearts and minds of his staff. The USA company has its own satellite TV station which beams programmes to its 50,000 employees. 'People respond to what they see and hear,' he says, 'not to what you write down.' He uses the TV to stress the value of the packages to people who are waiting for them and turns an ordinary delivery job into a real mission. He believes internal marketing is just as vital as external marketing.

Commitment can be an elusive quality. Roosevelt eventually roused the American people into discarding isolationism and joining the Second World War, but only because of the Japanese attack on Pearl Harbor. Ordinary people finally saw the dangers and opted to enter on the side of the allies. Unity created strength and this finally led to victory. 'Pearl Harbors' are sometimes necessary in teams, companies and countries. People are then more willing to commit themselves to achieving a common goal.

British people, for example, have a love-hate relationship with organisation. They want to retain their individual freedom, yet also enjoy the feeling of team spirit. These two drives can be married successfully. Churchill got people to pull together during the war, but failed during peacetime. The Bradford City fire, Zeebrugge and Kings Cross tube disaster showed how people can combine their talents to save life. Many times, however, people must have the knife at their throats before they work together as one team.

Let's look at one British success story. Pilkington plc are located in St Helens, Lancashire. They make good quality products and are a friendly company, with many people on first name terms. Pilkington's Insulation Division at their Ravenhead Works, however, faced a severe crisis in the early 1980s. World recession, oil price stabilisation and fresh competitors combined to reduce their share of the market. The financial year which ended in 1982 saw them projecting a loss of around £10m. One reason was their 'sales per employee' compared to that of their major competitors.

	Sales per employee
Pilkington	25K
Gypglas	55K
Rockwool	66K

Something had to be done. The company began by launching a reconstruction programme at Ravenhead. This package included leading from the top, communicating the vision, changing management attitudes, improving working practices and introducing flexibility at the sharp end. The painful part, however, involved reducing the work force from 1,800 to 500 over a period of three years. 'Creating ownership' was a challenge. How do you get people to own the process of making themselves redundant? Pilkington Insulation and the trade unions agreed on a common goal. The top team focused on changing management attitudes, while a Steering Group was set up to co-ordinate the restructuring process. This had 13 members from trade unions and only five from management. The job evaluation panel, which reviewed working practices, had a similar ratio. People approached the task seriously and found solutions to both the human and technical problems. It proved to be a good demonstration of teamwork. The company has survived. Restructuring was painful, but the alternative would have been worse. Management and trade unions can take credit for working together to achieve a common goal. Pilkington Insulation reduced their work-force to 500 by 1985. They also reported profits of £3.5m.

High-tech companies have a different culture from those born in the industrial era. You may have to offer different incentives to get commitment. John Sculley, for example, has an interesting view of how to win people in firms such as Apple. He believes people are looking for more than money; they are searching for a sense of mission. He writes:

They're looking for personal growth, for the chance to make an important contribution. They want to clearly understand the vision and direction of the corporation, why it's in business, and what that means to our society and view of the world. The trappings of loyalty – pension, cradle-to-grave employment – have been replaced by attention to such things as creating opportunities, rewards, and challenges for people. In return, people pledge their commitment to do their absolute best. For themselves and for the company . . . While I am not asking for

> *Leaders must know how to win the 'salt of the earth' people in the factory, office or street.*

open-ended loyalty, I am asking people who are at Apple to buy into the vision of the company while I am here.[1]

What's in it for me?' is the reaction of most people when presented with a brand-new sparkling vision. How can you inspire them to want to reach the mountain top? Some lessons are clear.

The leader needs:

- To present a positive vision;

- To show people that the pluses outweigh the minuses;

- To win the 'ordinary' people, particularly in large organisations;

- To present a clear strategy for reaching the goal;

- To show people that, providing they work hard, they can get positive results.

Imagine you work as a senior manager in a chain of motorway restaurants. Top management has reacted to years of criticism by deciding to upgrade the facilities. They aim to offer better quality food linked to better customer service. You have been invited to drive the service strategy through the company. Let's explore how you can get commitment from your people. You can follow similar steps in most teams, organisations or companies.

1: YOU CAN START BY WINNING YOUR IMPLEMENTERS

Who will you rely on? Let's assume you have five levels in the organisation: the frontliners, first-line managers, restaurant managers and district managers who report to you. (You may, of course, want to set up an implementation team to co-ordinate the customer service programme. We will look at this possibility in the next chapter.) But you will probably rely on two groups of people.

1 The district managers

They must inspire the restaurant managers to do good work for the company.

2 The restaurant managers

They must inspire the frontliners to do good work for the company.

Both groups need special attention. Involve them in developing the strategy, ask what support they need and demonstrate the rewards of focusing on customer service.

Key implementers can also come from the ranks of the unofficial leaders. Twenty years ago, for example, I was asked to run Lancaster House in Richmond, a therapeutic community for disturbed adolescents. We aimed to help young people to do what they want in their lives – providing they don't hurt themselves or other people. Allan and Toni were two 17-year-olds who had great influence over their peers. If we won these two leaders, they would win the rest of the group. We asked them to buy into the principles that underpinned the community:

- To change their life style – otherwise they and the other young people would continue to get into trouble

- To help other people

- To set and reach their personal goals

Toni and Allan chose to take this route. They stopped making excuses, found work they enjoyed and got some early successes. They acted as models for the other young people, who also became culture carriers. Lancaster House became known as a community that got results. Radio and television programmes about our work meant we got publicity and attracted more prospective residents. Allan, Toni and the other young people influenced the newcomers: they showed that being responsible could be successful. They became our implementers and made things happen.

Who are your culture carriers? They may be superintendents, foremen, line managers, a project team, captains on the field or unofficial leaders. How can you win them? Make a specific plan for encouraging them to buy into the vision.

2: YOU CAN PLAN HOW TO WIN THE 'ORDINARY' PEOPLE

Leaders must know how to win the 'salt of the earth' people in the factory, office or street. This is especially true in our post-industrial society because old assumptions, paradigms and working practices have to change. Ian Mitroff emphasises this point in his book *Business Not As Usual*:

Perhaps the most difficult part of the challenge is to alter the behaviour of millions of hard-working, competent, and conscientious Americans who have become used to, and good at, functioning in large bureaucratic organisations.[2]

You are in charge of the customer service strategy: how can you get commitment from the people who work at the motorway restaurants? Here are four suggestions.

Clarify the different target groups

List the different groups of people you must win. These may be, for example:

- District managers
- Administration staff at Head Office
- Restaurant managers
- First-line managers
- Chefs
- Waiters and waitresses
- Part-time cleaners

Clarify the pluses for each group

Find three selling points for each group. Why should the administrators, for example, commit themselves to customer service? They will have to ask what their customers – the restaurant staff – want and then provide it. They may also need to make life easier for people at the sharp end by changing their own work practices. Bureaucrats seldom enjoy losing power. But you need to find three pluses which are likely to win the administrators. What if there are no obvious pluses? People may even face the sack. As I will mention later, Hewlett-Packard tackled this problem in the 1970s and still managed to retain their staff's loyalty. However long it takes, find the pluses for each group. If they do not exist, you may have to create them to ensure there is a win/win solution. This part is difficult, but worthwhile.

You can clarify how to reach each group

Derek's work with the Olympic Basketball team, which I described earlier, called for more than team talks. He also met the 15 players individually for one-hour personal goal-setting sessions. Extra time was spent with the captain and unofficial leaders. Why? They were his 'coaches' on the field. He relied on them to make the system work, especially when times got rough.

Senior managers, however, won't have time to see each person on an individual basis. But it is possible to spend time with each group, to meet the administrators, to visit the restaurants and to stage a launch event. Internal marketing is like cultivating a field before sowing the seeds. If the ground remains hard, the seeds will not grow. Find the best way to reach the different groups of people.

3: YOU CAN EDUCATE YOUR PEOPLE ABOUT WHAT IS HAPPENING IN THE WORLD

Eric Nicoli, managing director of United Biscuits Brands, chose to tackle this and other challenges by introducing an attractive internal magazine called *Focus*. The name was chosen to emphasise the process of channeling the company's energies into reaching specific goals. He began by communicating the business vision:

> UB Brands will be the most profitable major operator within the [United Biscuits] Group and within its major markets through the motivation of its people and the satisfaction of its customers.[3]

UB Brands were already number one, so what was the problem? 'Change is the only constant' he wrote. Consumers were, for example, becoming more diet conscious. The company were introducing McVitie's Natural Choice – a selection of biscuits aimed to reach people who were concerned with 'healthy living and the importance of diet.' Apart from reinforcing the vision, *Focus* was used to highlight trends which might lead to changes inside UB Brands.

Motorway restaurants are subject to change. When launching the customer service initiative, it is useful to inform people about trends in the business. What are the company's strengths, weaknesses, opportunities and threats? Who are the potential customers? What do they want? Who are the competitors? What must the company do to improve their profits? Why choose customer service as a strategy?

One way to get 100% from your people is to give 100% to them.

What will this mean to different groups of workers? What will be the benefits? Make videos, write articles and hold teach-ins to inform people. They will then see what must be done to make the company successful.

4: YOU CAN CREATE OWNERSHIP

Standardisation is vital, but restaurants, like any other business, become soulless without the personal touch. Decisions should be made as far down the hierarchy as possible. People can be asked to generate their own ideas for improving customer service and encouraged to implement these changes. They can be asked what practical support they need and given it within two weeks. The company may also wish to consider introducing a scheme for profit-sharing.

As Robert Tomasko says in his book *Downsizing*, companies can create ownership even in bad times:

> In the early 1970s the entire electronics industry suffered a drop in orders, and most companies were laying off people in significant numbers. At Hewlett-Packard estimates indicated that it was necessary to cut back 10% in both output and payroll to match the decline in orders. In this company the obvious solution was to lay off 10% of the work force. Top management, however, was committed to avoiding lay-offs. After considerable discussion, a novel solution surfaced. Management decided to require everyone from the president to the lowest paid employee to take a 10% cut in pay and to stay home every other Friday. By distributing the 'pain' across organisational levels, Hewlett-Packard avoided both the human resources loss and the human costs associated with lay-offs.[4]

Everyone owned part of the suffering. They were then more likely to work together to create a better future.

5: YOU CAN COMMUNICATE YOUR VISION TO YOUR PEOPLE

Good leaders are good followers. They latch onto people's hopes, add their knowledge of the 'market place' and dare to 'educate' people a little. This is crystallised in a compelling vision and voiced in such a way that people respond by saying: 'We agree. We see the benefits. We want to do it.' How can you communicate your goal of achieving superb customer service? As I mentioned earlier in the book, we know it is useful:

- To communicate the vision in an exciting way;
- To create a one-sentence goal;
- To make the vision visible.

Winston Churchill, for example, knew how to use the media to rally the British people during the Second World War. 'We will never surrender,' was eventually replaced by 'Victory,' as the country's goal. He reinforced this message with management by walkabouts, radio speeches and two fingers raised in the 'Victory' sign to promise success. Churchill ensured everyone knew the goal: other leaders share their vision in other ways.

Montreal Canadiens (sic), for example, are one of the legendary ice-hockey clubs in North America. They owe much of their success to Frank Selke, who guided the club from 1946 until the mid-1980s. One employee recalls the first day he met their new leader.

'I'll never forget that day, August first,' says Camil Des Roches, who had begun working part-time for the Canadiens in 1938. 'Mr Selke walked into the Forum and very quietly let everyone know that he was the boss and would be the boss for a very long time to come. He did something that impressed me very much; he went around the whole building and introduced himself to everyone, ushers, carpenters, plumbers, ticket people. And from that day on, he always would have a hello and nice words for his people, no matter where they worked in the Forum.'[5]

Frank Selke demonstrated he had a clear goal for Montreal Canadiens. He then got loyalty from his people by broadcasting a message of commitment to his team. They showed loyalty to him for the next 40 years.

6: YOU CAN SHOW PEOPLE THE BENEFITS OF REACHING THE GOAL

You know the rewards for the administrators, restaurant managers, first-line managers, chefs and frontliners. These benefits may have already been communicated via articles, videos and small meetings. People will fight like hell to gain pleasure or to avoid pain. They feel motivated to give their best when they see some tangible rewards. Keep reinforcing the message.

Pilkington Insulation, for example, took their senior managers to a course centre for a three-day 'management dip'. The top team presented the vision, outlined the strategy and showed the pay-offs. Teams made their action plans and announced their plans for implementation. The 'dip' concept was repeated at different levels throughout the company. One year later the managers returned to review progress and look ahead to the future. They also presented videos of their own departments' successes during the past 12 months.

Rewards were thus made visible. These meetings reinforced the message: Pilkington Insulation were well on the way to building a winning team.

7: YOU CAN MAKE SURE PEOPLE KNOW THEIR PART IN REACHING THE GOAL

Everybody must know their role in the mission. Robert Tomasko underlines this point when discussing the ill-fated American attempts to rescue hostages from Iran.

> Israeli commando experts have been astonished that the United States mixed people with such different types of training, differing philosophies of warfare, and different career interests linked to their home services.
>
> For their successful hostage rescue at Entebbe, Uganda, the Israelis built a single, unified and elite team, completely separate from normal bureaucracy, with the shortest possible chain of command to carry out an extraordinarily difficult task. (Interestingly, entrepreneur Steven Jobs followed the same practice when he set up a skunkworks to design the Apple Macintosh computer.)[6]

Whatever the task – be it to rescue hostages, invent a computer or run a motorway restaurant – make sure everybody can describe their part in helping the team to reach its goal. Clarity creates confidence which in turn creates commitment.

8: YOU CAN EXPLAIN THE HARD WORK INVOLVED

Great leaders explain what people may encounter on the mission. Mother Teresa promises nothing to nuns who join her in Calcutta, except 'to give until it hurts.' Ernest Shackleton advertised in *The Times* for men to accompany him to the South Pole. He said there was no pay, terrible conditions and little prospect of return. He received hundreds of applicants. Florence Nightingale promised nurses nothing except a vocation in the Crimea. John F Kennedy said: 'We are going to put a man on the moon, not because it is easy, but because it is hard.' Winston Churchill promised nothing but 'blood, toil, sweat and tears.' People respect this honesty and respond to the challenge.

You are introducing a customer service strategy. What are you asking from people? To work harder; to work smarter; or to work more effectively? What are the minuses? You may be asking people to think differently. Psychological change, for instance, can sometimes be more threatening than physical change. Give people a full picture of the hurdles they face. Balance this scenario by explaining what will happen if the company fails to change. You cannot motivate people, they can only motivate themselves. People will respond to the challenge, if it's a worthwhile mission.

9: YOU CAN ASK FOR PEOPLE'S COMMITMENT

Leaders often guide people through three steps: encouragement, commitment, achievement. How will you ask people to take the second step? How will they demonstrate they want to give better service? Will you ask them to sign on the dotted line? Will you ask them to raise their hands? The Billy Graham model is appropriate when asking people to change their lives, but not when running a company. 'Silence is agreement' is a phrase used in some firms, but I doubt its value. One way to get 100% from your people is to give 100% to them. I suggest adopting a low-key approach. Allow time for discussion; then, unless disaster strikes, assume people are committed. Direct the energy towards a positive result. Ask people to suggest ways that: a) management can give them better service and b) they can give the customers better service. They will generate many concrete ideas which can be implemented. Follow up these ideas and produce some success signals within the next two weeks.

> *Clarity creates confidence which in turn creates commitment.*

Whatever method you choose you cannot persuade people to be committed; they have to opt in.

10: YOU CAN GET AN EARLY VISIBLE SUCCESS

Jan Carlzon changed the fleet's colours when he took over Scandinavian Airlines. Cabin crews were invited to design their own uniforms, planes were refurbished and the passengers were served better meals. SAS were suddenly in the headlines for the right reasons: planes flew on time and the company made a profit. Carlzon is a superb presenter and knows the value of making physical changes. Sometimes, however, the staff may need a shock to galvanise them into action.

Sir John Harvey-Jones, for example, made an immediate impact after being elected chairman of ICI. According to Barrie Ritchie and Walter Goldsmith in *The New Elite*, he said: 'I am a high-risk choice. What I am going to do may not work out. We failed to read the changing world in the 1970s. If I get it wrong again, I will resign.' Apart from reducing the board from fourteen to eight people, he made a symbolic move out of his office.

> Harvey-Jones abandoned the sumptuous boardroom with its huge round leather-covered table and its damask walls for all but formal, full-session meetings and transferred his executive team to a small lecture hall with individual desks. Suddenly a mutually congratulatory gathering of the mighty was transformed into a battle briefing of fleet commanders.[7]

He demonstrated something was happening. Harvey-Jones changed the physical to change the psychological to change the philosophical. ICI updated their logo, introduced family days and urged staff to be more entrepreneurial. Leaders may get early visible results, but the next step is serious implementation.

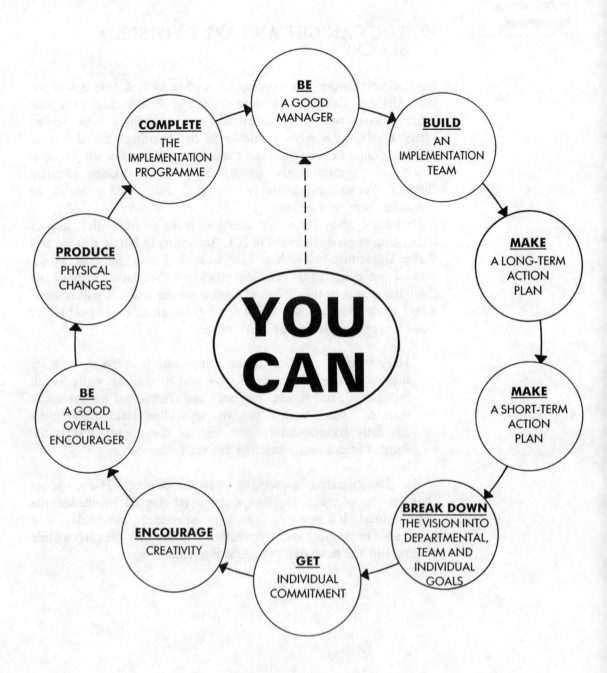

Chapter 6

HOW TO BE A POSITIVE IMPLEMENTER

How can you make things happen? Peter Ueberroth faced this challenge when he organised the 1984 Olympics in Los Angeles. He had to raise money from sponsors, fix venues, arrange travel, oversee security, ensure the events ran smoothly and, finally, overcome the Soviet boycott. How did he do it? He began by setting up two implementation teams.

'I believe in leadership and trust. People with those two qualities can manage anything,' writes Ueberroth, in his book *Made in America*.

> It was with this in mind that I conceived the commissioner programme, a sports management technique new to the Olympics. Each of the 23 Olympic sports was to be run by a commissioner whose function was chief operating officer . . . I flipped through my Rolodex for men and women I knew and I had seen in action over the years. By the summer of 1983 I had filled every position.[1]

The generals were in place, but who would be the foot soldiers? He recruited an army of 70,000 volunteers who were willing to give up a month of their time to enjoy a once-in-a-lifetime experience. These frontliners would make or break the Games. Ueberroth had some doubts about their ability at first, but was swung by his wife's argument.

> Ginny had been involved with several volunteer organisations over the years and was a firm believer. 'Once volunteers get behind a project, they'll stick with it to the end – they'll be the best employees of all,' she added.

The Los Angeles Games were pronounced a financial and sporting success, despite the Soviet boycott. One journalist wrote after the opening ceremony: 'The first gold medal has already been awarded, even before the games have begun. It goes to Peter Ueberroth.' Ueberroth disagreed. He said the gold medal should go to the volunteers who dealt with the everyday nitty-gritty.

Implementers translate an ideal into reality. Business and sports don't have a monopoly on such people. Britain, for example, has produced many social pioneers. Elizabeth Fry introduced penal reform. Dr Barnardo set up homes for children. Florence Nightingale created a nursing force in the Crimea. A S Neill gave birth to Summerhill School. Alec Dickson started Voluntary Service Overseas and Community Service Volunteers. Peter Benenson founded Amnesty International. All translated their words into action.

IBM are a company who have traditionally expected their middle managers to be implementers. The top team provides the vision; their job is to convert these words into physical actions. The middle manager's role is:

- to commit themselves to the company's beliefs and follow them in practice,
- to translate the company's vision into action, build successful teams and get positive results,
- to inspire, develop and keep people in the company,
- to develop their own talents and continue to serve the company.

IBM realise that the third and fourth points have become increasingly important. Why? The quality of the company depends on the quality of its people. Middle managers must create a supportive and stimulating environment, because 'problems with the boss' is a frequently cited reason for leaving many other companies. Thomas Watson Snr recognised this potential danger, invested in management education and created an environment which bred loyalty. IBM still offer superb training to their middle managers. They do, however, have an ageing work-force who are being asked to update their skills. The company are also making great efforts to attract and keep younger staff.

Good implementers do the simple things well. You have been asked to improve the motorway restaurants by introducing better customer service. We have already explored ways to get commitment, but let's go back to basics. You may want to begin by clarifying your own service philosophy. Here is one view of what should happen in such a programme.

CUSTOMER SERVICE

- Start by giving good service to your colleagues and staff.

- Educate your staff to give good service to the customers.

- Recognise your customers' expectations and moments of truth.

- Verify and improve the four Ps in the service package: the people skills, products, practices and packaging.

- Implement the service programme and achieve visible results.

- Check you are achieving customer satisfaction.

- Encourage your staff by rewarding them and celebrating success.

How can you translate this into action? Here are ten steps you can follow to make things happen.

1: YOU CAN BE A GOOD MANAGER

Implementers gain respect by acting as good models. Peter Ueberroth, for example, built his company, First Travel Corporation, from nothing into the second largest travel organisation in America. Business people admired his success and trusted his ability to run the Los Angeles Olympics. They showed this by investing in sponsorship. He gained respect from the volunteers by 'living the message' and being an excellent manager. As an implementer, it can be helpful to master the following basics.

Manage yourself

Make sure you are doing the right job at this time in your career. Spend quality time by yourself, with your family and at your work. Stay healthy and treat yourself occasionally. Spend time with your encouragers. Laugh a lot and retain a sense of humour.

> *The quality of the company depends on the quality of its people.*

Manage your time

Structure your time in blocks. Make clear action plans. As Alan Lakein said: 'Keep asking yourself: "What is the best use of my time right now?" ' Use the 80/20 rule. Get to meetings in time. Always let people know if you will be late. Write less, telephone more. Handle each piece of paper once only if at all possible.

Manage the practical tasks

Be a good organiser. Make sure all the practical tasks get done in an enjoyable and effective way. Be clear on all the jobs that need to be done and the talents of the people in your team. Get people to do what they enjoy doing and do best. Share the remaining tasks to everybody's satisfaction.

Manage your meetings

Make sure the meeting is necessary. Have clear objectives and invite only the necessary people to attend. Agree on the agenda. Be clear about what can and can't be discussed at the meeting. Deal with the easiest items first. Ask people to speak one at a time. Encourage them to present possible solutions, rather than problems. When discussing items, be task-oriented. Keep asking: 'What is the result we want to achieve?' Summarise the action steps to be taken and finish on a positive note.

Manage your people

Recruit the best, give them the best, expect the best. Provide positive leadership and build winning teams. Listen to people, encourage them and give them space to be creative. Be results-oriented and make sure they deliver. Getting the best from your people will mean getting the best from your business.

2: YOU CAN BUILD YOUR IMPLEMENTATION TEAM

Apart from yourself, who will drive the strategy of improved customer service? The top team will provide support, but don't rely on the cascade system. Middle managers will usually do their best and become valuable allies. Messages can become distorted and diluted, however, if they are passed down the company and hit pockets of resistance. The best bet is to build a team who have responsibility for driving the programme. They can run courses, co-ordinate people's suggestions and produce visible results. Who should be in the team? Line managers make superb implementers. They have worked at the coal-face and can gain respect from their colleagues. Don't select 'evangelical pioneers' who are likely to upset others. Here are some rules for choosing people to be in the team.

- They should be loyal to the company. They should also believe in the company's strategy, which in this case emphasises 'service'.

- They should have 'street credibility'. They should be respected by the board, line managers and frontliners.

- They should be good at internal marketing and have a flair for public relations.

- They should be good listeners, communicators or teachers. They should be able to 'listen downwards', speak to the staff in their own language and give flesh and blood examples from the work-place.

- They should be good managers who can implement ideas and produce physical results. They should also be looking for a challenge and want to serve the company.

You will also be relying on managers at every level: the district managers, restaurant managers and supervisors. They are your captains and coaches on the field. As I mentioned earlier, your first message to them is: 'Start by giving good service to your own colleagues and staff.' Live the message in your own work. Support them, tap their knowledge and use their ideas. They will determine whether or not the customer service programme is successful.

3: YOU CAN MAKE YOUR LONG-TERM ACTION PLAN

You will probably make two kinds of action plans, whether you are running the customer service programme, the Olympic Games or any business. The first action plan will resemble a long-term road map: it will show all the jobs which must be done during the entire project. Some people love to draw every step before setting out on the journey: other people prefer to start hacking at the jungle. You will create your own type of long-term plan for the project.

Football managers, for example, are action men. They love to get their heads down, sweat and produce quick results. This approach is great: providing they know their destination, start out in the right direction and deliver the right results. Some years ago, I ran courses for football managers at the Swedish National Sports School. My job involved teaching management skills and offering them a season-long road map. I am including the check-list in an appendix because it demonstrates one kind of detailed long-term action plan.

4: YOU CAN MAKE YOUR SHORT-TERM ACTION PLAN

Nitty-gritty jobs must be tackled in the next day, week and month. You need to make telephone calls, design booklets, make videos, win the district managers over, organise course accommodation, set up meetings, etc. People make different kinds of short-term action plans. Some use elaborate systems, others use the back of an envelope. People must find their own method. The only real test is: does it work?

The next pages offer one model for both long-term and short-term goal-setting. Some of the questions are obviously not necessary when, for example, you compile a daily 'to do' list. If this is the case, simply go on to the second part and write down, for example, five things you want to do in the next week. It can be useful, however, to return occasionally to the four key questions to ensure you achieve the right results.

Frank Selke, for example, sprang into action on the day he took over Montreal Canadiens. Apart from having a long-term aim, he set short-term goals which produced a visible result. Thirty-seven years later he recalled his reaction upon walking into the stadium.

> I'll never forget that first afternoon at the Montreal Forum. The place was filthy and the stench of poorly managed urinals knocked you down when you opened the front door. I had come from the working-class and I would not stand for sloppiness at any level. The local fans deserved to sit in comfort and enjoy a high quality of entertainment, so my first task was to invest more than $100,000 in a new plumbing system and undertake major renovations in the buiding.[2]

Selke believed his first responsibility was to the customers who paid for their tickets. He aimed to welcome families to the Forum, so it must be clean and attractive. Like Sir John Harvey-Jones and Jan Carlzon, he carried out a short-term action plan which made an immediate impact.

HOW TO SET POSITIVE GOALS

You can ask yourself:

1: WHAT IS THE RESULT I WANT TO ACHIEVE?

- You can say: 'I want to . . . '

- You can choose one goal and make this super-specific.

- You can describe this in behavioural terms.

- You can describe what will be happening that will tell you that you have reached your goal.

2: WHY DO I WANT TO REACH THE GOAL?

- You can be clear on the rewards of reaching the goal.

- You can see how reaching the goal fits into helping the company to reach its goal.

- You can describe the pluses and minuses and make sure you really want to reach the goal.

- You can get the 'What?' and 'Why?' right before moving onto the 'How?'

3: HOW CAN I DO MY BEST TO ACHIEVE THIS RESULT?

- You can say: 'I can . . . ' and brainstorm lots of ideas.

- You can go for quantity rather than quality and have a wide repertoire of possibilities.

- You can then be selective to be effective and go for quality rather than quantity.

- You can choose the methods most likely to succeed.

- You can make a back plan.

4: WHEN DO I WANT TO BEGIN?

- You can say: 'I want to . . . ' and make a concrete action plan.

- You can set your success criteria so that you can check that you have reached your goal.

- You can make sure that you are prepared to pay the price needed to reach the goal.

- You ask for the support you need in order to reach each goal.

- You can commit yourself to reaching the goal.

- You can go on to making plans for reaching the next goal.

FIVE THINGS I WANT TO DO IN THE NEXT WEEK

1 I WANT TO . . . .

2 I WANT TO . . . .

3 I WANT TO . . . .

4 I WANT TO . . . .

5 I WANT TO . . . .

5: YOU CAN BREAK DOWN THE VISION INTO DEPARTMENTAL, TEAM AND PERSONAL GOALS

Peter Ueberroth provided an overall picture for running the Los Angeles Olympics. The leaders, teams and individuals then took responsibility for their own particular areas, such as: sponsorship, security, accommodation, travel, the opening ceremony and television coverage. The vision was translated into reachable goals and followed up by making action plans.

People in charge of any project – be it customer service, quality management or any business – must clarify the goals on many different levels. You can, for example, clarify what must be done by the top team, district managers, restaurant managers, supervisors and frontliners. Break down the vision into departmental, team and personal goals. Clarify what people can do to achieve these goals.

The restaurant managers, for example, have to translate the service strategy into physical actions. How can they move from theory to action? The following service mnemonic provides an overview of the steps you want the managers to take, but this isn't enough. They must break down these phrases into concrete action plans. Legendary service, however, calls for people doing things with passion. Before they will put their hearts into their work, there is an even more vital step – getting their individual commitment.

THE CUSTOMER SERVICE STRATEGY

S tart by giving good service to your colleagues and staff.

- Provide a positive vision.

- Live the message.

- Ask the staff what support they need and give it to them.

- Do that little bit extra.

E ducate your staff to give good service to the customers.

- Show the reasons for giving good service.

- Show it is the customer who pays the wages.

- Show what is happening in the world.

- Show the rewards in giving good service.

- Get their ideas for improving the service.

R ecognise your customers' expectations and moments of truth.

- Ask the staff to find out what the customers want.

- Ask the staff to plot the customers' way through the system.

- Ask the staff to record the customers' moments of truth.

- Organise the work to give the customers what they want.

V erify and improve the four Ps in the service package: the people skills, products, practices and packaging.

- Be clear on the four Ps you offer in the service package.

- Find concrete ways to improve the people skills.

- Find concrete ways to improve the product.

- Find concrete ways to improve the practices: to put the customer first.

- Find concrete ways to improve the packaging.

Implement the service programme and achieve visible results.

- Get the staff to 'own' the service programme.

- Get them to plan how to implement their concrete ideas in specific areas.

- Go for guaranteed visible successes.

- Do things which will immediately show staff and customers that something is happening.

Check you are achieving customer satisfaction.

- Take specific steps to check the results.

- Ask the customers: 'What are we doing right? What can we do better and how?'

- Incorporate their ideas in a programme of constant improvement.

Encourage your staff by rewarding them and celebrating success.

- Record your ongoing achievements.

- Set a date for celebrating success.

- Give your staff real and tangible rewards.

- Continue following this pattern – which takes us back to the first step. Start by giving good service to your staff and colleagues.

6: YOU CAN GET PEOPLE'S INDIVIDUAL COMMITMENT

Now comes the crunch. You know what must be done by the top team, district managers, restaurant managers, supervisors and front-liners. How can you get them to want to do it? How can you inspire the restaurant managers, for example, to be good coaches for the supervisors? You can't always tell people what to do: you need their hearts, souls and energy. We've already explored how to reach large groups: how can you reach individual people? Three guidelines are helpful:

> *Implementers gain respect by acting as good models.*

- Show people what needs to be done.

- Involve people in dialogue goal-setting.

- Agree on each person's individual commitment.

Performance management sessions, for example, are one tool you can use to encourage people, develop their talents and agree on common goals. Such programmes must meet four conditions if they are to be successful.

1 They must be presented properly inside the organisation.
2 They must be seen as a positive experience for almost everybody.
3 They must be simple and easy to understand.
4 They must lead to positive results.

IBM took this path many years ago: they do, after all, believe in management by commitment. Companies that fail to take sufficient care when introducing performance management will encounter enormous problems. The first step, then, is to introduce the system. The second step is to run the actual sessions. Such meetings work best, I believe, if people prepare properly. They should also be warm, future-oriented and involve dialogue goal-setting. The list below describes ten steps you may wish to follow during a session on performance management. Earlier in the book I mentioned taking these steps with Per, my centre-forward in the Swedish football team. Let's explore these again, because you can use a similar model in the work-place. Two weeks before our meeting, I asked Per to write his goals for the forthcoming season. I also invited him to make two lists headed: 'Three things I do well as a player', and 'Two things I can do even better – and how'. At the same time, I wrote my views on his performance, plus my goals for him as a player. We then met for one hour to discuss the lists and integrate the two sets of goals for the season. We began by looking at Per's view of his strengths and areas for improvement. I then shared my view of what he did well. The next step was to consider his goals for the season. While encouraging Per, it was also my job to help him to see the whole picture. I outlined what I wanted him to do as a centre-forward and we agreed on common goals. I then asked Per what support he needed, made clear contracts and got his commitment to reaching the goals. The final step was to work together to achieve these results both on and off the field.

Whether you lead footballers, restaurant managers or frontliners, management by commitment calls for dialogue goal-setting. Show people the whole picture. Involve them by inviting their suggestions. Agree on common goals and provide 100% support. People will then be more likely to *want* to reach their targets.

HOW TO RUN A PERFORMANCE MANAGEMENT SESSION

Here are ten steps you can go through during the session. Each of these could, of course, be gone into in greater detail.

1: You can prepare properly for the session.

2: You can get the 'human' part right during the session.

3: You can make a clear contract for the session.

4: You can look together at what the person does well, what they can do even better – and how.

5: You can look together at the person's previous goals and results.

6: You can look together at the person's career plans – and get their ideas for improving the work-place, customer service and organisation.

7: You can agree on the person's specific goals – and link these to the team goals.

8: You can ask what support the person would like to do the job and say what you can and can't give.

9: You can use 'What? How? When?' to make an action plan and agree on clear contracts.

10: You can follow up the session and work together to achieve positive results.

7: YOU CAN ENCOURAGE PEOPLE TO BE CREATIVE

The implementation team can create enthusiasm and co-ordinate the staff's ideas for improving the business. Balance 'hands-on' with 'hands-off'. People will produce literally hundreds of suggestions. You want them to feel excited, but you can't have 'hares running all over the place'. How can you tackle this challenge? Make clear contracts by explaining the areas they can and can't influence. This will designate the borders within which they can make changes. You can offer people different techniques they can use to generate ideas. Staff can be given a creative tool box which includes tools such as brainstorming, right brain and left brain activities, mind mapping, visualisation, suggestopaedia, neuro-linguistic programming (NLP) and synectics. Encourage them to express, rather than suppress, their talents. Innovation is fine, but ensure ideas are implemented. Publicise success stories, because this will inspire other people to be creative.

8: YOU CAN BE A GOOD ENCOURAGER

Ken Blanchard, author of *The one minute manager*, suggests 'catching people doing something right'. This involves seeing what a person does well and telling them immediately. Why? Positive strokes can give people the strength to tackle both challenges and set-backs. Tell the district managers what they do well, for example, and they are more likely to support the restaurant managers. One of them may eventually write a note saying:

> Yesterday I received a call from the Blue Line coach company to congratulate the M4 restaurant on how they had looked after a coach-load of old-age pensioners. Several of the party felt ill on arrival and the staff responded by opening up a special room in the restaurant, providing waitress service and departing from the set menu to provide special food. Apparently this included scrambled eggs on toast, Horlicks and cream buns. The coach company do not expect this kind of treatment every time, but they were impressed by the way you responded to the crisis. My thanks to all the staff for doing that 'little bit extra'.

'Service is our business' is a way of life, rather than a slogan. The way the staff are treated shapes the way they treat the customers. Encourage the district and restaurant managers and they will encourage the supervisors and frontliners. This will pay off in the bottom line when they give good service to the customers.

(There is also a time for 'tough love': giving a person very clear messages about what you expect them to do better in the future.)

9: YOU CAN PRODUCE PHYSICAL CHANGES

Brian Spicer's TQM team at BA workshops invited the engineers to improve their work-places. Each shop floor team were given the autonomy they needed, for example, to design better benches, consult directly with third party customers and change their practices. This resulted in greater job satisfaction and increased performance.

You can, for instance, introduce a positive polaroid exhibition. Robert Townsend makes the following suggestion to managers in his book *Further Up the Organisation*:

Polaroid Power

If you are responsible for a group of hamburger stands, service stations, banks, nursing homes, or supermarkets, where appearance is critical, take a polaroid camera along on your trips. If you seen an obsolete sign, a dirty counter, or a slovenly employee, take a picture. Show it to the manager. Tell him it will be prominently featured in your rogues' gallery back home until he sends you a picture of the new look.

Worth a thousand words? More like a million.[3]

Why not reverse the idea? Photograph the improvements in motorway restaurants, for example. Staff may well build adventure playgrounds; employ a part-time clown to entertain the children; keep the areas spotless; improve the food; provide an indoors play area; set up information desks; lease areas to travel agents, sock shops and other franchises; keep the toilets clean, etc. Capture each team's successes and include these in an ongoing positive polaroid exhibition.

10: YOU CAN COMPLETE THE IMPLEMENTATION PROGRAMME

Peter Ueberroth's job was almost over when the last athlete left Los Angeles. Despite the Soviet boycott, the Olympic Games had made a profit. Security hadn't been breached and many people were left

> *Recruit the best, give them the best, expect the best.*

with happy memories. Reflecting on the volunteers' achievements, he wrote:

> We had climbed the mountain together. It was long and hard and as we approached the top the air became thinner; it became painful for everybody. Coming down was equally painful. I knew many would want to stay there; others would look for other mountains. I wished them all well but warned each that there would never be another mountain like organising and staging the Olympic Games.[4]

Implementers are good finishers. You can fulfil your brief and complete the programme on customer service. Finishing provides a great feeling, but it turns sour unless people have done good quality work. Let's look at how they can take this step towards reaching their goals.

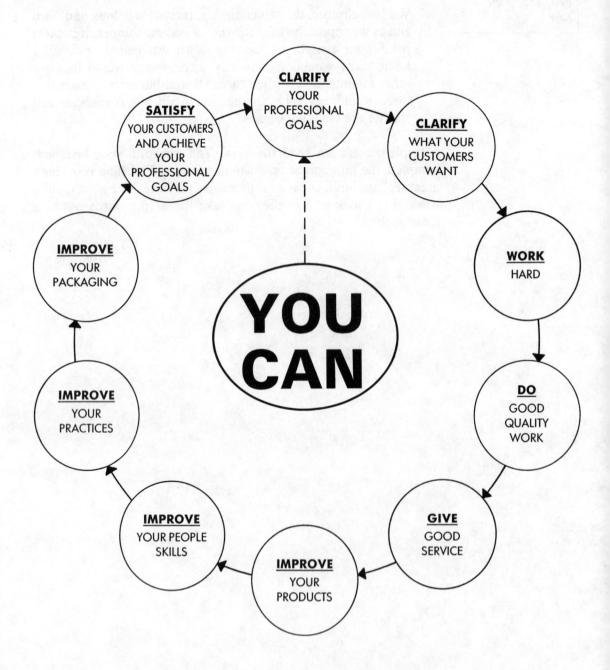

Chapter 7

HOW TO DO POSITIVE WORK

David Attenborough has translated his love for nature into wildlife series such as *Zoo Quest*, *The Living Planet* and *Life on Earth*. Apart from providing entertainment, his BBC TV programmes have highlighted threats to the rain forests and endangered species, such as the giant panda. He follows his passion, produces excellent products and helps to build a better planet. This is what I call positive work. People often follow five guidelines toward doing such work.

- They do work they love.

- They find out what their customers want.

- They do good quality work.

- They achieve customer satisfaction.

- They do this to achieve a profit for themselves and for the planet.

Can people follow such idealistic rules in the hard world of business? Let's take a look. People who take a pride in their job are those who do work they enjoy. This applies to artists, teachers, shop owners, pilots or truck drivers. Federal Express, for example, aims to give service which is 'legendary'. People who do work they love have a quality-check in their guts. They automatically do that little bit extra. Passion plus professionalism equals peak performance.

Theodore Levitt once said, 'The purpose of marketing is to create and keep a customer.' Advertising won't succeed, however, unless firms supply quality products and services. Companies must build a long-term marriage with their customers, rather than indulge in a one-night stand. Konosuke Matsushita, founder of the company whose brands include National Panasonic, underlines this point. He says:

> After-sales service is especially effective if you act before the customer complains about your product or something goes

wrong with it. For example, when summer approaches and people take out their electric fans, just drop in at the houses of customers who bought fans at your store last year. Say 'hello', and ask how the fan is working, then check the fan and clean it. I call this 'hello' service. The service is free, of course. There is no immediate profit. But the customer is pleased and his or her trust in you goes up by a large percentage. For the businessman, there is no greater happiness and sense of worth in your work than what your customers' delight and their trust in you can give.[1]

Anita Roddick's story, for example, contains as much business-sense as it does idealism. It has been told many times before, but it is worth exploring again, because it highlights the concepts of what Barrie Hopson and Mike Scally call the four Ps[2]. The Body Shop stocks quality products. The staff learn people skills: they are, for example, urged to give information rather than to 'sell'. The company displays good practices: it designs shops, for example, which are user-friendly. The packaging is simple and attractive: it appeals to people who want to purchase the products. Let's go back to the beginning.

'Think like an immigrant', is the advice given to many budding entrepreneurs. Anita Roddick had such models. Her Italian parents ran an American-style 'diner' café in Littlehampton. As Gilly McKay and Alison Corke say in their book about the Body Shop:

> Italians have a tradition of giving good 'service'. Whereas the surrounding English-owned cafés closed at 5 pm, they stayed open until the last customer had gone and then opened at 5 am in the morning for the fishermen's breakfast. From her parents' enterprise, Anita learned to provide a service in response to people's needs, and to create an atmosphere conjured up by an almost theatrical set-design.[3]

She introduced these qualities into her first shop, which opened in Kensington Gardens, Brighton. Work is about people, products and profits, in that order: so she faced a challenge when franchising the Body Shop. People who applied for a franchise had to be ethical, know their customers and see retail as theatre. Anita wanted to maintain the company's special culture. She adopted a 'hands-on' approach at the first franchises in Bath, Hove and Bognor Regis. This became impossible as more shops opened, so she set up the Body Shop's training college in 1984. As Gilly McKay and Alison Corke say: 'Most of all, the training courses are designed to motivate shop staff with enthusiasm for the Body Shop philosophy, and give them pride in their work'. Anita Roddick continues to run courses at the college and visit the shops. Like many good leaders, she stays in charge of the company.

People often follow similar steps to do good quality work: whether they run the Body Shop, lead National Panasonic or produce a wildlife series. Let's put this to the test. Imagine the BBC have invited you to step into David Attenborough's shoes. They have asked you, for example, to make a 30-minute TV programme on polar bears. Similar steps can be taken whether you make a film or do good work in your own team, organisation or company. Let's take a look at these steps.

1: YOU CAN CLARIFY YOUR PROFESSIONAL GOALS

First, clarify your philosophical goals. Kahlil Gibran once said: 'Work is love made visible'. Do something you believe in which makes a contribution to life. Grand words are fine, but translate them into action. Convert your ideals into practical goals. If you make a polar bear film, for example, your overall professional goals may be:

- To build a good project team.

- To make a good film about polar bears.

- To get a good response from the viewers.

- To get a good response from your bosses.

- To do work which has a good effect on the environment.

These can be broken down into more specific goals, but let's move on to the next step. Certain rules hold true, whether you make a film, run a school or design a computer. If you want to get paid for your work, you must integrate your own vision with that of your paying customers.

2: YOU CAN CLARIFY WHAT YOUR CUSTOMERS WANT

Henry Pluckrose, former headteacher of Prior Weston School, stayed close to his customers. Parents, for example, recalled their own first day at school and getting lost in an army of children. They wondered if anything could be done to help newcomers to the school. How could he solve the problem? Each child now visits the school several times before his or her official first day. They are also the only one starting school on that day. Teachers know the child's name, give them special attention and integrate them into a small family group. Henry knew how to satisfy the parents who ultimately paid his wages.

Back to the polar bear film. You have at least two sets of customers: your bosses and your viewers. Start with the television viewers. Who is your target group? Get to know your audience. Discover what they want to know about polar bears. What kind of film would be most appealing: 'A day in the life', 'The polar bear's life-cycle' or 'The kingdom of the ice bear'? What similar films on this subject have been produced or are in the pipeline? How can you be sure to capture the television audience? What would make your polar bear film special? Get to know your audience's wishes and needs. Clarify your vision. Check this with the BBC bosses and ask about their goals. They may wish, for example, to attract an audience of seven million viewers, sell the programme to ten networks and publish a book. Listen to their ideas and integrate them into the final vision. You are paid to do a job, but don't be afraid to 'educate' your bosses, in the nicest possible way. Agree on 'what' is to be achieved and by 'when'. It's up to you 'how' you achieve this vision. Fight for your creative freedom, but be prepared to be judged by your results. Get the support you need and make a clear working contract. Move on to the next step.

3: YOU CAN WORK HARD

Sebastian Coe has worked hard both physically and mentally to reach his goals. He experienced one of his darkest hours after competing in the 800 metres at the 1980 Moscow Olympics. Steve Ovett had taken the gold and Coe felt like packing his bags and flying home. He had beaten himself. He allowed himself to be boxed in during the race and 'only' won a silver medal. Did he have the mental toughness to compete at the highest level? Did he have the hunger and courage? Seb won his own personal battle and took charge of the 1500 metres final. He triumphed over his own doubts and the opposition to win the gold medal.

Whether you want to win a race, make a film or tackle any project, there are at least three key aspects to doing hard work.

Make an action plan

Creativity, we are told, calls for 90% perspiration and 10% inspiration. Organisation is also vital. The polar bear film will need planning in great detail. You may need:

- to set aside three months of your life to shoot the film;
- to make a story-board showing the format for the programme;
- to write a provisional script;
- to organise the money;
- to recruit the project team;
- to find shooting locations in the Arctic;
- to organise the transport and book accommodation;
- to shoot the film;
- to edit the film and provide the commentary;
- to write the book to back up the series;
- to make a set of learning materials for schools;
- to arrange the publicity;
- to launch the film;
- to respond to viewers' letters;
- to follow up with talks which show people how they can make a contribution to caring for the polar bear and its environment.

Spontaneity takes a lot of planning. Structure also provides the freedom to take the next step.

Do effective work

Barrie Pearson offers an interesting view on this subject in his book *Common Sense Business Strategy*.

> People confuse work with results. Work in fact is often allowed to become an obstacle to achieving outstanding results. Many executives spend most of their time doing work which could be done at least as well and more cheaply by one of their staff. Not

surprisingly these are the people who complain that they do not have time to invest in the future success of the business.

Chief executives, business owners and partners in professional firms must make time to create a vision of success for their business. They need to define the future direction of the business in terms of commercial rationale and priorities. The issues which are crucial to the success of the business must be identified and tackled vigorously. Work must not be allowed to get in the way of future success.[4]

Be selective to be effective. Do the right things right and, if possible, do them right first time. Nothing will, however, help you to get around the next step.

Be prepared to sweat

Many people, for example, dream of writing a book. They have this picture of themselves signing their latest best-seller for queues of admiring fans. But the writer's life can be one of great labours; getting up in the morning, facing a blank page and words dropping like blood on to the paper. It can also be one of lightness, joy and easy flows. Some say that the only thing worse than writing is not writing. People need to work hard – and enjoy the journey – if they are to produce their books.

We will return to the polar bear film in Step Ten. For the moment, however, let's explore several aspects which can be integrated into any kind of work.

4: YOU CAN DO GOOD QUALITY WORK

Quality is meeting customer requirements. One year ago, for example, you may have bought a Japanese TV from a store in the High Street. Would you pay the same price again for the same product from the same company? If so, you have purchased quality.

You can't tell people to produce quality; they have to want to do it. It starts with them doing work they love, whether they are writing a book, cooking a meal or fixing an aircraft engine, they must have a gut feeling for their work and take a pride in their efforts. In order to make a profit, they must also achieve customer satisfaction.

Harland & Wolff, Xerox and Toshiba are among the firms which have introduced total quality management. This calls for meeting the requirements of both their external and internal customers. It calls

> *Spontaneity takes a lot of planning. Structure also provides the freedom to do effective work.*

for improving their people management, as well as their products, practices and packaging. Companies that do this will get commitment from their people and repeat business from their customers.

Every quality management programme is unique. Some embrace the whole philosophy of Kaizen and dedicate themselves to constant improvement. They must, however, be introduced in a way that fits the culture, rather than imposed from outside. Good programmes have three characteristics: they have commitment from the top, create a sense of ownership, and achieve visible results. Harland & Wolff, Xerox and Toshiba have found quality management leads to improved performance, products and profits.

5: YOU CAN GIVE GOOD SERVICE

Service is part of the overall business strategy. When two companies offer identical products, the one which offers the better service will keep the most customers. Good service means meeting customer requirements and giving people a little bit more than they expect. One key element is to recognise how the customer makes their way through your business system – and then to improve upon it. When someone travels by air, for example, the customer's activities will include:

- finding the airline's telephone number;
- telephoning to make the reservation;
- travelling to the airport;
- carrying their baggage through the airport;
- finding the airline's desk at the airport;
- picking up their ticket;
- finding the check-in desk;
- standing in line to check in themselves and their baggage;
- going through passport control;
- going through the security check;
- waiting in the departure lounge;
- waiting for the flight to be announced;
- making their way from the departure lounge to the gate;

> *Be selective to be effective. Do the right things right and, if possible, do them right first time.*

- waiting again to board the aircraft;
- squeezing along the aircraft corridor to find their seat;
- finding a place to stack their cabin luggage;
- waiting for the aircraft to take off;
- enjoying or hating the take-off;
- taking off;
- waiting for the in-flight meal;
- enjoying or disliking the in-flight meal;
- getting to the toilet;
- enjoying or hating the landing;
- struggling to get their luggage from the overhead rack;
- waiting for people to disembark;
- walking to the passport control;
- waiting for their luggage to arrive;
- getting through customs;
- looking for their transport to their destination;
- journeying to their destination.

The airline that helps people to negotiate these moments happily will attract the most repeat business. As Jan Carlzon said, SAS's task was not to get one thing 1,000% better, it was to get 1,000 things 1% better. Let's take a deeper look at these twin concepts of quality and service.

6: YOU CAN IMPROVE YOUR PRODUCTS

Merck was voted the most admired pharmaceutical company by American executives in 1988. Why? For at least two reasons: they are honest and they produce quality products. As Doug MacMaster, the company President, says:

> It made good sense to be ethical. To tell the full truth about your product makes you all the more believable. Our success in selling is really based on very good products and having tremendous credibility.[5]

It pays to offer value for money. Some examples are the BBC's natural history programmes, the Volkswagen Beetle, Marks and Spencer clothes. Commercial success also calls for business sense. The old adage remains: don't try to sell a Rolls-Royce to someone who can only afford a Mini. Make sure you make a profit; otherwise you will not have the money to stay in business. The Japanese, of course, aim to attract and keep customers for life. Not content with this, they aim to reach the next generation. If the whole family is satisfied with our car, they reason, the children are more likely to purchase our cars in the future. As Konosuke Matsushita points out, the physical product is just one part of the package. He writes:

> After-sales service is the key to keeping your customers. No matter how good the product you put on the market, if you do not provide equally good after-sales service, the customer will not come back. He will shower you with complaints and then go elsewhere. In many respects service is more important than the product itself. If you cannot provide good after-sales service for all the products you offer, you should consider reducing your range from five product lines to three, for example. In the long run, it is better to reduce the scale of business and achieve perfection in the quality and servicing of a smaller number of products. A manufacturer who cannot do that much defaults on his responsibility towards his customers.[6]

7: YOU CAN IMPROVE YOUR PEOPLE SKILLS

Everyone has a horror story about bad service. Many of these stories result from encounters with cashiers, bank tellers, telephonists, waiters, hotel receptionists and airline personnel. In the eyes of the customer, the frontliner *is* the company. If this person has bad people skills, the whole company suffers. It has been calculated that a customer needs 12 positive experiences with a company to make up for one negative encounter.

Good service is often accompanied by excellent people skills. The hotel receptionist, for example, may have greeted you warmly, given you a choice of rooms, offered to book your airline ticket and used your name when handing you the room key. Maybe s/he has been on a charm course. Providing the words are backed up with real help, however, you will be left with a good impression.

Let's look at the people skills involved in enabling the customer to enjoy their plane journey. A good airline will analyse the customer's moments of truth and make sure they receive satisfying service. The check-in person, for example, needs:

- to enjoy working with people;
- to be well organised;
- to welcome people;
- to get the first ten seconds right;
- to look and sound pleasant;
- to use good body language;
- to give their full attention to one person;
- to be a good listener;
- to show they understand the person's request;
- to answer any questions about flights;
- to allocate a seat;
- to communicate simply and clearly;
- to label and dispatch the baggage;
- to know how to deal with stress;
- to display grace under pressure;
- to make each person feel special;
- to show flexibility;
- to deal with any problem people;
- to make reassuring signs to other impatient passengers;
- to get the last ten seconds right with the passenger;
- to remember that the last thought lingers longest;
- to keep an overall picture of what is happening;
- to help other people in the team;
- to welcome the next passenger.

People skills like these have to be repeated throughout the air journey. But they alone do not comprise good service. They must be backed up by the next step.

8: YOU CAN IMPROVE YOUR PRACTICES

Good practices call for putting the customer first, rather than last. In other words, designing the system to fit the customer, rather than forcing the customer to fit into the system. This highlights two aspects of service.

You can develop good working practices

Banks, for example, are rapidly introducing new technology which enables them to respond quickly to their customers. They are also installing more cash machines which reduce queues and cut down on waiting times. This releases frontline staff. They are being trained to talk with the 'new' customer: a target group that is more sophisticated about money, less afraid of debt and made up of an increasing percentage of women.

Apart from updating their technology, banks have to update their human awareness in order to stay in touch with their customers. Providing an efficient and friendly service is the only way they will stay in business.

Airlines can improve their working practices. Two recent economy class flights I took illustrate how two sets of cabin crew tackle the job of serving the in-flight meal. One was excellent, the other was like a scene from the Marx Brothers, except nobody was laughing.

The SAS cabin crew were well organised. They served the meal and wine together, then offered passengers warm bread rolls. After a suitable period they toured the aircraft with more warm rolls and offered tea and coffee. People were allowed to finish their meal in peace before the cabin crew collected the empty trays.

Cabin crew in Airline 2, however, had a different idea. They served the meal 30 minutes into the two-hour flight. People who wanted wine with their food had to wait a further 20 minutes. When the wine trolley appeared, the cabin crew began collecting the empty trays of people who had grown impatient and eaten their food. They dropped dirty cutlery on to people's laps, offered wine or coffee, and cast dark looks at those who hadn't finished. Chaos reigned and the remaining passengers began rushing their meal. We were thanked for choosing their airline and it was hoped we had enjoyed a pleasant flight.

They could certainly improve their working practices.

You can develop good customer practices

Put the customer first. Airline 2's cabin crew, for example, needed to make life pleasant and easy for the passengers, rather than forcing them to fit into their system. Banks must also take this step. They need to have friendlier opening hours, develop home-banking and ensure their 'older-style' managers know how to talk with the 'new' customers.

Sometimes you can invite the customer to take part in the transaction. Many large stores, for example, have educated the customer to participate in the service. Leaflets containing nutritional information, recipes and serving suggestions are to be found in most supermarkets nowadays, so the unsophisticated customer feels more knowledgeable and the store does not have to pay someone to pass on this information.

9: YOU CAN IMPROVE YOUR PACKAGING

Airlines provide a similar product: a journey from A to B. The only thing that differentiates them is the way the service is packaged. British Midland, for example, have their own passenger lounge at Heathrow's Terminal One. This gives people a chance to relax away from the milling crowds who are waiting for domestic flights run by British Airways and Air UK. They have also introduced Diamond Class which offers excellent food, free newspapers, etc. Some people will say this is just wrapping. They are right, but the way a package is wrapped can make it more delightful for the receiver. Airlines often package their products to reach a certain target group. Adverts aimed at business people, for example, stress door-to-door limousine service, easy check-in, preferential treatment, private lounges, working space and leg room, superb service, peace, the chance to catch up on sleep and punctual arrival. Airlines are continually seeking the competitive edge and this is one of the few ways they can stand out from their competitors.

TV series are the leading edge when it comes to packaging. Once upon a time there was just the programme itself. Now the BBC, ITV and Channel 4 realise there is a lot of mileage in producing trailers, a book, videos and learning materials. BBC Enterprises, for example, have been set up to capitalise on this and earn much-needed money to supplement the licence fee.

10: YOU CAN SATISFY YOUR CUSTOMERS AND REACH YOUR PROFESSIONAL GOALS

Back to the polar bear film. How can you incorporate the four Ps in your work? Apart from giving people pleasure, this will increase your 'marketability' in the future.

Your product

You can make a quality film which is entertaining, educational and effective. It can match both your own and your customers' expectations. Try to include that 'little bit extra' which makes it stand out from other natural history programmes.

Your people skills

These will be needed when making the film. Apart from motivating your staff, it will be useful to get on with the locals when shooting on location. You may need to be good at 'talking into the camera' to reach viewers in their living rooms. When marketing the programme, you will need to meet journalists and get your points across in interviews and articles.

Your practices

Adopt good working practices when shooting the film. Make the work enjoyable, but ensure it is effective. Polar bears won't repeat catching a seal if the crew weren't ready. Good customer practices are necessary if you want lots of viewers to see the film. Fight for it to be shown at peak-time and ensure it is well advertised. Get the first five minutes right so they don't switch to another channel.

Your packaging

Produce attractive trailers and articles which capture the viewers' imagination. The book and video can be described as ideal presents for birthdays or Christmas. The sale of polar bear calendars, tee-shirts and posters can finance educational materials for schools.

These can include work-books about protecting the Arctic and caring for the earth's environment.

How can you check that you satisfy your customers? There are at least five ways.

- You can get the viewing figures. This will reveal the number of people who saw the programme.

- You can commission a viewer's poll to check how they rated the programme on a scale of 1 to 10, where 1 is low and 10 is high. Find out what people liked, what could have been better and how. This will reveal the quality of the film.

- You can check with your film crew. How did they rate the final film on a scale of 1 to 10? What could have been better and how? This will reveal the professional's view.

- You can check with your bosses. How did they rate the film on their priority scale? What was good? What could have been better? This will give you the employer's view.

- You can check with yourself. How did you rate the film on a scale of 1 to 10? What was good? What could be better and how? This will match your original vision with the reality.

If you want to satisfy yourself, it is vital to reach your professional goals. If you want to earn a living, it is vital to satisfy your customers. This brings us to the next step: to build a positive reputation.

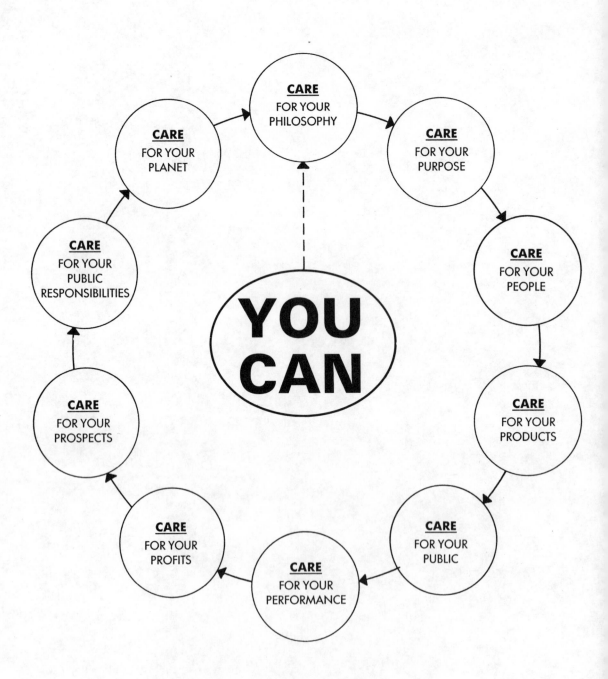

Chapter 8

HOW TO BUILD A POSITIVE REPUTATION

Good organisations care for their people, products and planet. Maybe this sounds old-fashioned in these money-conscious days, but many companies are turning principles into profits. Let's look at some of them.

Johnson & Johnson, for example, faced a crisis of public confidence in 1982 when several batches of Tylenol capsules were injected with cyanide as they lay on supermarket shelves. Seven people died in Chicago and this created panic. The company responded by recalling the product and introducing a 'tamper free' package. Even this did not work and some of the new packages were injected. The company responded by turning to its written credo. The first line read: 'Our first responsibility is to the doctor, nurses and patients, to mothers and all others who use our products and services.' Instead of stalling or lying, it was obvious what to do. They withdrew the products, even though this cost them $150m. Why? One answer is that it made long-term commercial sense. Drug manufacturers realise there is nothing worse than to have a dirty reputation. Another answer is that Johnson & Johnson took their values seriously. Lawrence Foster, their vice president, pointed out they had been telling their staff for 40 years that they were expected to follow the credo. The company were now on trial in front of the nation. If they tore up their principles during the Tylenol crisis, the credo would have looked a sham. They really had no choice. Three months later a poll showed that 93% of the public felt Johnson & Johnson behaved responsibly during the crisis. Tylenol also regained its place in the market. This episode, however, was neither the beginning nor the end of the story. Since the early 1970s the company has held 'credo challenge meetings' in which they have tested their ideals against hypothetical crises. The company's written ideals have made both moral and commercial sense. J & J have followed them and gained respect for their actions.

What about caring for your people and products? Marks and Spencer have a long track record in this respect. They were, for example, among the first to give their staff in-store restaurants, foot-care facilities and profit-sharing schemes. The St Michael brand has become a sign of value for money. 'If it isn't good enough for me and my family to eat or wear, it isn't good enough for us to sell,' said Marcus Sieff. Caring for their customers also means providing an instant exchange or cash refund for any faulty item.

Caring for your products calls for being a good model in your own work-place. Richard Norman illustrates this point in his book *Service Management*. He paints such a graphic picture that it is worth quoting at length.

> Suppose that a customer enters a restaurant and orders a dish from the menu. Let us also suppose that he is neither very knowledgeable nor very discriminating about food, and that he is a one-time visitor who is just passing through the town. Suppose that just today the restaurant happens not to possess the perfect faultless ingredients needed for this particular dish – it is a bit of a gamble whether it will be up to standards or not. The chef hesitates but decides to serve the dish. He may have done a fine job; the normal standard may have been exceptionally high; or the customer's lack of knowledge and low standards have come into play; but, whatever the reason, our customer walks away happy and satisfied. So everything is all right? No, because something extremely significant has happened: a new norm has been established in the company, stating in effect that 'it's all right to cheat the customer a little, especially if he doesn't seem to notice.' The customer may not notice, but there is no way of hiding what goes on from the employees. In the end, the service itself will be affected – and finally the customers will notice.[1]

What about caring for the community? British Airways are building bridges with other parts of society. One challenge they face, is helping their engineering apprentices to learn teamwork. How can they get these 'hard' guys to learn the 'soft' people skills? One solution: they ask teams of apprentices to organise and run a one-week holiday for mentally handicapped young people. Apart from learning to work in teams, they learn the joy of giving to other people. BA's initiative has proved to be an outstanding success for both them and the community.

What about caring for the planet? 3M, for example, have a programme called 3P: Pollution Prevention Pays. This was intro-

> *Good organisations care for their people, products and planet.*

duced in 1977 and encouraged employees to develop projects for preventing pollution. One proviso: they must save or make money. This has proved more than window-dressing. John Elkington and Tom Burke describe the results in their book *The green capitalists*:

> By 1983, for example, a total of 52 projects had been accepted for 3M's programme in the United Kingdom, bringing savings over six years of more than £2.25m. Altogether, those projects eliminated 3,150 tonnes of air pollutants, 830 tonnes of sludges and solid wastes and 34 million gallons of contaminated water. Worldwide, nearly 1,000 3P projects had made or saved £77m.[2]

Enlightened self-interest? Yes, of course. Business people want to continue making money, but they can only do this if we still have a planet. 'Yes, but many industries are still doing harm', argue some people. This is true, but the tide is turning. Many companies have the heart, knowledge and power needed to improve the environment. 3M and IBM are among those that are doing practical work to care for the planet. Such companies often follow certain steps:

THE POSITIVE COMPANY

- They care for their Philosophy.
- They care for their Purpose.
- They care for their People.
- They care for their Products.
- They care for their Public.
- They care for their Performance.
- They care for their Profits.
- They care for their Prospects.
- They care for their Public Responsibilities.
- They care for their Planet.

What about your own team, organisation or company? How can you continue to create goodwill? Here are ten steps you may wish to follow.

> *Caring for your products calls for being a good model in your own work place.*

1: YOU CAN CARE FOR YOUR PHILOSOPHY

Thomas Watson Jr, the former chairman of IBM, stressed the importance of the company having a philosophical backbone, or a set of three basic beliefs: 'respect for the individual, service to the customer and excellence in everything we do'. Why these? Because, he said, if we treat people well and satisfy our customers, this will lead to increased personal commitment and profits. Reinforcing this message, he wrote:

> I firmly believe that any organisation, in order to survive and achieve success, must have a sound set of beliefs on which it premises all its policies and actions.
>
> Next, I believe that the most important single factor in corporate success is faithful adherence to those beliefs.
>
> And finally, I believe that if an organisation is to meet the challenges of a changing world, it must be prepared to change everything about itself except those beliefs as it moves through corporate life.[3]

IBM was a byword for these things until the 1970s. At that stage it became bureaucratic and lost touch with its customers. Bad results during the mid-1980s forced the company to return to its basic philosophy. The first step was to get out of the plush office, become street-wise and relearn how to respect the modern individual. Why was he or she choosing to buy from Apple or Digital? What did the new customer want? The second step was to provide real service and achieve customer satisfaction. The third step was never again to lose touch with their basic philosophy. IBM regained some of their profits, but still have some way to go to regain their former reputation.

As we have seen, Johnson & Johnson reached for what they believed in when faced with the Tylenol crisis. They went back to their values and put them into practice. Whatever your philosophy, there will be times when it is sorely tested. Ken Blanchard and Norman Vincent Peale tackled this subject in their book *The Power of Ethical Management*.[4] They suggested asking three questions before making a difficult decision.

First: is it legal?

If it isn't, decide whether or not you want to cheat and/or commit a crime. Sports authorities, for example, must enforce the rules and not tolerate people breaking the laws. The German Football Association, for instance, refuses to stop their players cheating. Their

Many companies have the heart, knowledge and power needed to improve the environment.

national players frequently roll around the floor as if they are experiencing death agonies after receiving a hard but fair tackle from an opponent. As a flagrant attempt to get a fellow professional sent off, this has no place in the game.

Second: is it balanced? is it win/win?

Good negotiators say it is vital for both partners to emerge with something from a settlement, even if it is only their dignity. Blanchard and Peale say that win/lose solutions become self-defeating: whether it is in daily life, business or marriage. The winner is happy for a time, but the loser starts looking for revenge. Pain, depression and ongoing fights eventually turn this into a lose/lose situation.

Third: how will it make you feel about yourself?

Is it something you will be proud of doing? Would you like to see it published in tomorrow morning's newspaper? This is the acid test. How many people would have remained faithful to their wife/ husband if they knew that their one night stand would be publicised in the next day's paper? How would they feel facing their partner and children?

Blanchard and Peale suggest running ethics workshops where managers use these questions as a framework for making decisions. Companies that have a written credo and hold such workshops are then more likely to put their principles into practice.

2: YOU CAN CARE FOR YOUR PURPOSE

Viktor Frankl believed that people need to have more than a philosophy of life, they need to have a purpose. They need to have a mission, vision and goal. Konosuke Matsushita believes companies should follow a similar rule. He says:

> Every company, no matter how small, ought to have clear-cut goals apart from the pursuit of profit, purposes that justify its existence among us. To me, such goals are an avocation, a secular mission to the world. If the chief executive officer has this sense of mission, he can tell his employees what it is that the company seeks to accomplish, and explain its raison d'être and ideals. And if his employees understand that they are not working for bread alone, they will be motivated to work

together toward the realisation of their common goals. In the process, they will learn a great deal more than if their objectives were limited to pay scales. They will begin to grow as people, as citizens, and as businessmen.[5]

What is your company's purpose? What is the purpose of your school, hospital, government department, factory or office? Is it to educate children, to help people heal themselves, to serve the citizens, to make plastics or to make a profit? If you work for a business, for example, try to fill in the following lines.

The purpose of our company is:

1 To . . . .

2 To . . . .

3 To . . . .

4 To . . . .

5 To . . . .

Teams work well together when they have a common purpose, whether it is climbing Everest, tackling the effects of an earthquake or inventing a computer. Discuss your list with your colleagues, agree on the top three priorities and put these on a poster. Hang this on the wall and make sure you follow it every day. This will give you even greater strength to tackle your daily work.

3: YOU CAN CARE FOR YOUR PEOPLE

This should be a 50/50 working relationship. While the company should encourage its staff, the staff should care for the company. After all, it is the company that pays their wages and, ultimately, their food, mortgages and holidays. As John Young, president of Hewlett-Packard, once said:

> The HP Way really begins with a belief in people. We offer opportunities for meaningful participation in a team effort, but only to people who take responsibility for themselves. We aim

for a naturally self-motivating environment, and we depend on people to do their jobs right.[6]

John Welch, chief executive of General Electric, echoes this view. He believes the job of the enterprise is to provide an exciting atmosphere that's open and fair, where people have the resources to go out and win. The job of the people is to take advantage of this playing field and give 110%. As I have mentioned elsewhere, there are five good ways to care for people in an organisation.

Thomas Watson Jr, the former chairman of IBM, stressed the importance of a company having a philosophical backbone, or a set of three basic beliefs: 'respect for the individual, service to the customer and excellence in everything we do'.

You can support the positive majority

Encourage the people who are willing to build a 50/50 relationship with the company. It is 'false caring' to pander to people who are not willing to take responsibility for their actions and/or break the rules.

You can give people the support they need to do the job

Follow up the beautiful words with concrete actions. Give people the encouragement, tools and incentives they need to do the job.

You can share the rewards

Done in the correct way, this gives people a sense of ownership and motivates them to work even harder. Sharing the fruits of their labours can be profitable for both them and the organisation.

You can support the people behind your people

Take care of your staff's families. Invite their children to look around the building; send them presents, diaries and models; hold a family day.

You can show people they are part of one team

Ensure people have a sense of unity. Help them to see how every department plays a part in achieving the goal. People will then give even the 'Cinderella' department the respect they deserve.

4: YOU CAN CARE FOR YOUR PRODUCTS

Jens Nielsen, director of design for the Danish State Railways, takes a pride in his products. He loves his work and believes design is 'values made visible'. Anyone who has travelled on his country's trains and ferries would say his company has done a good job. This wasn't always the case as he mentions in his book:

> Nowhere is design – good or bad – more in the public eye than in a railway company. For years the Danish Railways had been a motley mixture of the ancient, unchanged and haphazard . . . So it was clear from the start that the designer's job would be to strike a balance between creativity and the need for a tight planning rein. He would have to be something of a gardener: encouraging growth here, pruning bits there. Always with an eye on the overall effect.[7]

Nielsen's design team have certainly achieved this goal. The stations are neat, attractive and clean; the cafés are welcoming, comfortable and pleasant; the signposts are well-placed, easy to read and informative. The Danish railways are, he believes, like arteries that link towns, span waters and join together a somewhat scattered country. They are the life-blood of the nation and create a sense of unity. As such, they deserve the best design.

Good design is simple, beautiful and effective. Are you proud of your products? Do they achieve these criteria? Choose one of them and find three ways to improve it. This is one to value your own work and give value to your customers.

5: YOU CAN CARE FOR YOUR PUBLIC

Corporate giants have sometimes been reluctant to look after the customers who keep them in business. Ford, for example, had to experience heavy losses between 1980 and 1983 before they saw the light. The top brass then became committed to producing quality. Christopher Lorenz charts their progress in his book *The Design Dimension*:

> Ford had to undergo a conversion of Galileo-like proportions. Conventional wisdom in the automobile industry had always put a company's interests before those of its customers. 'But that has changed,' declared Donald Petersen (the new chairman), 'now the driver and passengers, not the company, are the center

'*Every company, no matter how small, ought to have clear-cut goals apart from the pursuit of profit, purposes that justify its existence among us. To me, such goals are an avocation, a secular mission to the world.*'
Konosuke Matsushita

of Ford's universe.' If the result was a set of products that made Ford markedly different from its competition, that would no longer be a worry – in fact, so much the better. Never mind if their low noses, high tails and smooth shapes quickly earned them the nickname of the 'jelly-mould look'.[8]

The results paid off. Ford found that the Sierra and Scorpio/ Granada became big hits with the customers and reversed the downward trend. Caring for the public was also rather profitable.

My local bank showed another way to look after their customers. Christmas was approaching and they knew that people would become impatient standing in longer queues. What to do? Apart from installing an electrical queuing system, the bank provided seats, coffee and biscuits for people waiting for their number to be shown. Nobody could ignore the frustration felt by the customers, but it could be eased a little.

How can you care for your public? Try to find three concrete ways. Put one of these into practice each week and you will build a positive reputation.

6: YOU CAN CARE FOR YOUR PERFORMANCE

Peter Vidmar, Olympic Gold Medallist in the Los Angeles Games, now makes a living describing ways to achieve peak performance. He does this by referring to his own discipline of gymnastics. In a lecture entitled, 'ROV: the key to a perfect 10', he starts by talking about the hard work that goes into reaching Olympic standard. He then outlines the scoring system in competitions. When performing on the parallel bars, for example, your marks would be made up in the following way:

9.4 To gain this you must reach a supreme level of *professional competence*. Only then will you receive this mark.

0.2 To gain this you must take a *risk*. You do not have a choice whether or not to take one, you must.

0.2 To gain this you must show *originality*. You must do something that has never been done before.

0.2 To gain this you must show *virtuosity*. You must carry out your discipline with flair and star quality.

Providing you do all of these things superbly, you will achieve your perfect 10. Peter brings along his own set of parallel bars and

> *The job of the enterprise is to provide an exciting atmosphere that's open and fair, where people have the resources to go out and win.*

gives the audience a demonstration of how to do all these things. He finishes by saying: 'So work hard, dream dreams and take risks. You can do it.' People feel uplifted and burst into great applause. Although Peter has mentioned it several times, it is doubtful whether many people actually hear what he said. They like phrases such as 'Believe in your dreams – Be original . . . Go for it.' But the ROV part of a gymnast's performance is only 0.6. The athlete has to start by getting the 9.4 right in terms of professional competence.

The same rule can be applied to any job. There is the constant need to get the basics right – to get the 9.4 right – and to strive for perfection. As a football manager, for example, there is only one thing harder than getting a team to want to improve after a defeat – that is getting them to want to improve after a win. Caring for your performance calls for maintaining your professional competence, then adding risk, originality and virtuosity.

7: YOU CAN CARE FOR YOUR PROFITS

There are different kinds of profit. If you work in a hospital, it will be measured in terms of health and human happiness. If you work in a school, it will be measured in terms of student and parent satisfaction. If you work in a business, it will be measured in terms of staff morale and financial success. Caring for your profit means doing everything you can to get good results. It calls for using money effectively, improving work practices and being prepared to sweat. After reaching your targets, it calls for investing your profits wisely.

Henry Pluckrose believed Prior Weston School, for example, should enable children to gain self confidence, knowledge and an appreciation of the arts. Providing the staff did their job properly, and kept their eyes on the target, the children would reap these rewards. Henry made sure everybody benefited from the experience: the students, parents and staff. Because it was well run and reached its goals, the school gained a good reputation and built a long waiting list. In this sense, Prior Weston was a profitable enterprise.

Companies, of course, are obsessed by the bottom line. There are three reasons for making money in a business. The first is to pay your bills. This is a matter of survival. The second is to pay your shareholders who have financed the firm's growth. This is a matter of moral duty. The third is to invest for the future. This is a matter of innovating in order to maintain employment.

George Gilder stressed the need for companies to keep in touch with their entrepreneurial roots in his book *The Spirit of Enterprise*. He believed this was necessary if people were to retain a moral and healthy attitude to money, otherwise they could become hooked on trying to get rich for the sake of getting rich. He wrote:

> Entrepreneurs understand the inexorable reality of risk and change . . . Their chief desire is not money to waste on consumption but the freedom and power to consummate their entrepreneurial ideas . . . By the very process of acquiring profits, they learned how to use them. By the very process of building businesses, they gained the discipline to avoid waste and the knowledge to see value. By the process of creating and responding to markets, they orient their lives toward the service of others.[9]

Companies need to educate their people about the need to make a profit. They also have to use the financial rewards in a moral way. Providing the team, organisation or company reaches its 'profit' target – be it goodwill, health or financial rewards – they must invest it wisely. This takes us to the next step.

8: YOU CAN CARE FOR YOUR PROSPECTS

Richard Foster describes why this is vital in his book *Innovation: the Attacker's Advantage*. 'As much as 80% of all manufacturing industries and a large portion of all service industries will see major technological changes before the year 2000.'[10] There are at least three ways you can care for your future.

You can invest in your people

The Abbey National building society, for example, invested in a two-day customer service programme for all of their staff called 'You Are The Difference.' It emphasised just that point: people like to buy from people, not from faceless institutions. Apart from the frontline effect, this kind of course forms part of internal marketing. Skilled employees are becoming more choosy and realise they are in a sellers' market. Companies must do all they can to attract and keep good quality people. Those that do so will maintain a competitive edge in the future.

You can invest in your products

The advent of the Walkman and digital watches shows the value of innovation. They changed the paradigm and kept their companies ahead of their competitors. It isn't enough, however, to have a good idea. Turn-around-time, re-tooling and delivery are equally important. The company or organisation that can market an idea first is the one which gains an advantage. Those that fail to do this will become modern-day dinosaurs.

Consolidation is also vital. Ask yourself: 'What are our present best-sellers? How can we make more income from them?' This helps to create a good economic foundation for the future. Some companies are so much in love with invention that they fail to capitalise on their present products and this leads to their downfall.

You can invest in your public relations

BA Engineering, for example, are spending more time visiting local schools to meet the students. They describe the airline's work, give away aircraft models and interest them in the company. Why? One reason is that the number of school-leavers applying for apprenticeships is shrinking dramatically. Apart from visiting schools, they are inviting magazine journalists and taking every opportunity to appear on television and radio. BA have to attract more high quality young people in order to maintain their standards.

9: YOU CAN CARE FOR YOUR PUBLIC RESPONSIBILITIES

Levi-Strauss is one of the many US companies who care for their local community. Apart from providing grants, they provide people and expertise. This has led to their building community involvement teams (CIT) who work on improving the quality of life in their local community. Here are some examples of their work:

> In Charleston, South Carolina, Strauss workers developed plans and fund-raising events in support of a hospice for the terminally ill. In Boone County, Kentucky, a CIT landscaped and installed playground equipment in a new children's park.[11]

What do you think about your local school: is it good, average or bad? How can you help to make it even better? British firms are

Design is 'values made visible'.
Jens Nielsen

building bridges with educators but still have a long way to go to match what has happened in America. As John Naisbitt wrote in *Reinventing the Corporation*, in 1984 there were over 10,000 corporations involved with around 20,000 schools. The 'Adopt-A-School' programme, for example, was especially popular. Companies linked up with local schools and worked out a programme based on their needs. Employees taught classes, acted as role models and involved students in their own work-place. Some examples:

- Chase Manhattan Bank set up a management training institute for principals.

- Fairchild Industries bring high school seniors into their board-room as junior directors and hire teachers for part-time summer jobs.

- Bechtel, Shell Oil Co., and IBM have sent technical staff to work with students at their adopted schools.

Federal Express' involvement with a High School in Memphis, Tennessee, was so successful that it led the principal to say that it was: '. . . The best thing that has ever happened to Booker T Washington and I mean that. It has the most telling effect that any kind of community agency or outside agency has ever had on the school – period.'[12]

10: YOU CAN CARE FOR YOUR PLANET

Volkswagen has set up a 'greener' factory in Germany. Mazda is producing a hydrogen car which emits vaporised water rather than fumes. Tesco, Sainsbury and Gateway are beginning to introduce a more environmentally friendly approach to the siting and stocking of supermarkets. European regulations will ensure that more companies clean up their acts. Business people are starting to care for the ozone layer, rain forests and dying lakes. They are even working alongside environmentalists to create win/win solutions. The stakes are high: the continuation of human life on the planet.

What can you do in your company? You can start by following the surgeon's motto: 'First, do no harm.' You can then set aside a percentage of the profits to clean up the countryside, plant trees or improve another aspect of the environment. You can then consider adopting the ideas suggested by John Elkington and Tom Burke in their book *The Green Capitalists*. Here are ten ways they believe your company can develop environmental excellence:

> *Consolidation is vital. Ask yourself: 'What are our present best-sellers? How can we make more income from them?'*

1 You can develop and publish an environmental policy.

2 You can prepare an action programme.

3 You can organise and staff the programme.

4 You can allocate adequate resources.

5 You can invest in environmental science and technology.

6 You can educate and train your people.

7 You can monitor, audit and report on their programmes.

8 You can monitor how the green agenda is evolving throughout the world.

9 You can contribute to environmental programmes.

10 You can help to build bridges between the various interests.[13]

3M's three P programme is unique but I believe people in business will play an increasing role in cleaning up the environment. Why? They have the vision: they can see what is happening. They have the power: they are good implementers. They have the rewards; they want to continue doing business on this planet. Companies will, for their own survival, become even better global citizens.

Whether it is in caring for people, products or the planet, good leaders want to build a positive reputation. Why? To attract high quality staff, to take a pride in the work and to satisfy their customers. They are then more likely to take the next step. Good leaders help their people to achieve positive results.

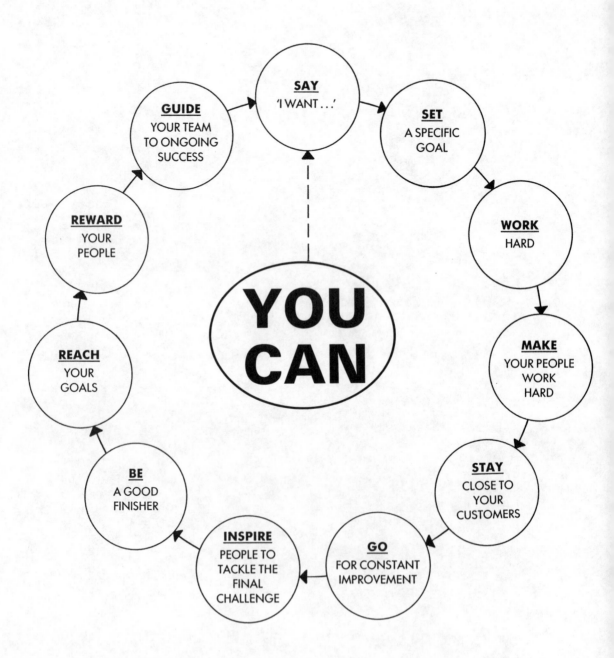

Chapter 9

HOW TO GET POSITIVE RESULTS

Peak performers are good finishers. Sebastian Coe, for example, knows that the 1,500 metres is decided on the last lap. In the Los Angeles Olympic Games he got his tactics right, dictated the race and led into the final bend. Steve Cram was one metre behind and made his final effort. Coe redoubled his efforts, sprinted ahead of the other athletes and went for the gold medal. He aimed beyond the tape and didn't start celebrating until the job was done. Finishing is vital: whether you are running a race or leading a business.

Leaders command respect by getting results. Anita Roddick is listened to because she produces profits and a well-motivated staff team. Franklin Roosevelt was revered because he introduced the New Deal. Dag Hammarskjöld was well regarded because he restored some credibility to the United Nations. Lord King and Sir Colin Marshall are admired because they turned around British Airways. In the world of leadership, nothing succeeds like success.

Pioneers sometimes take a long time to reach their goals, whether they work in business, social movements or any walk of life. Thor Heyerdahl's mission, for example, began when he visited Tahiti in 1937. He asked himself several questions. Could the Incas have travelled from Peru to Polynesia via the Pacific? Could they have sailed 4,000 miles on a balsa wood raft, the only technology available to them at the time, to Easter Island? Kon-Tiki was the old Peruvian sun god, while there was a Polynesian god called Tiki. Was there a connection? Could he prove it by making a similar journey? The Second World War interrupted his explorations.

Heyerdahl resumed his quest in 1946, but raising money proved difficult. Experts said the balsa wood craft would absorb water and sink into the ocean. He eventually financed the venture through personal loans, chose a team of five friends, and then travelled to Peru. The crew built the Kon-Tiki, a replica of the Incas' craft, and set sail for the Pacific Islands on 28 April, 1947. Storms, encounters with sharks and losing people overboard accompanied their three-month journey. The South East Trade Winds finally drove the

Kon-Tiki past jagged rocks to run aground on the Raroia atoll on 7 August. Heyerdahl faced a further challenge. He wrote a best-selling book which caught the public's imagination and paid off his debts. But the academic experts remained unconvinced about his theory. The Norwegian responded by writing a serious study in 1952 called *American Indians In The Pacific* and charting a trawler to take a team of archaeologists to Easter Island. The evidence they produced finally persuaded the scientific community that the Incas had travelled from Peru to Polynesia. The academic community gave his theory the seal of approval at the Tenth Pacific Science Conference in Hawaii in 1961. Heyerdahl had taken 24 years to reach his goal.[1]

Whether you are leading an ocean expedition, computer company or hospital team, it is vital to reach your targets. Let's take a look at the art of finishing: first, how to finish as an individual; second, how to finish as a team. The first part is easier because you rely on yourself. The second part is harder because you have to rely on other people. That, however, is what this book is about: inspiring people to achieve positive results.

HOW TO FINISH AS AN INDIVIDUAL

Every person is born to finish something. Frank Lloyd Wright's mission was to design houses. Martha Graham's mission was to found a famous dance company. David Attenborough's mission is to make wildlife films. What were you born to complete during your life?

'I never finish anything,' said John. He was employed as a social worker and didn't see a visible product in his work. But this was a matter of scale, because he had already completed at least 100 things that day. That morning, for example, John had woken up, switched off the alarm clock, climbed out of bed, brushed his teeth, cooked breakfast, got dressed, walked to the car, started the engine and driven to his destination. Maybe these are little things, but in each case John had followed the same four steps toward reaching his target. He had said: 'I want . . . ', set a goal, worked and finished. He could follow the same guidelines whether he was cleaning the dishes, painting a picture or trying to change the world. Let's look at how you can take similar steps toward completing a job.

1: You can say 'I want . . . '

One way to start is by making a list headed: 'Five things I want to finish in my life.' Write down your hopes and dreams. Maybe you

> '*Routine suffers from a bad press . . . Routine creates an area of time which is to be regularly occupied in a certain way until further orders.*'
> Jean-Louis Sevan-Schreiber

want to write a book, raise a family, travel to America, run a guest house in Cornwall or climb the Matterhorn. Try doing the exercise on this page. Do not censure anything: get all your ideas into open.

FIVE THINGS I WANT TO FINISH IN MY LIFE

I want . . .

1 To . . . .

2 To . . . .

3 To . . . .

4 To . . . .

5 To . . . .

2: You can set a specific goal

The key is to work on your A1 priority, so list your goals in order of priority. Creative people start many projects but only finish a few; so do not worry if you do not complete every job you tackle. This does mean saying 'Yes' to one dream and 'No' to others. But you have to concentrate your energies on one thing if you are ever going to finish it. If your A1 goal seems too far out of reach, concentrate on one that is easier to achieve.

Choose a specific project. Describe what you want to do and why you want to do it. You may write, for example: 'I want to publish a beautiful book about how to build a positive school. Why? Because this will encourage teachers and give hope to future generations.' Make your goal even more concrete by drawing a picture of yourself completing your book. Why? Because many people must actually see themselves finishing before they can reach their goal.

3: You can work hard

Good planning will help you to succeed. You have to write the book first, but your real goal is to publish it and help future generations. Start by exploring the market. What kinds of books are being written

> *Good leaders offer people a sense of hope and ownership.*

about positive schools? Who are the publishers? What about desktop publishing? If you choose this path, how will you market it? Create as much certainty as possible before you proceed. You will never get enough, that is the artistic reality, but researching possible outlets for your book will give you the confidence to start writing. What about the nitty-gritty business of doing the hard work? Break down the task into manageable lumps and get into a routine. The same rules apply whether you are writing a book, building a house or trying to change the world. Jean-Louis Sevan-Schreiber describes this process in his book *The Return of Courage*. He says:

> Routine suffers from a bad press . . . Routine creates an area of time which is to be regularly occupied in a certain way until further orders. The practice of cutting down carries out a similar prescription but is applied to a single task which otherwise would be to much for me. I haven't the courage to sit down and write a book, but perhaps I have enough to write four pages a day which, in 50 days, comes to 200 pages. With a bit of cunning we can almost always cut a task into pieces small enough for us to handle without pain.[2]

Here are some tips for tackling your project. You may need to develop your own strategies for success.

- You can do the jobs you enjoy.

    Start by doing the jobs you like best – or which you feel are most necessary. Perhaps you want to make the outline for each chapter, collect anecdotes or find cartoons to illustrate to book.

- You can structure your time.

    Set aside a block of time in which to do the job. Start on one job at a time and keep going until you have completed it. You will then feel successful.

- You can set short-term goals.

    Look ahead and make plans for the next day. Set a realistic goal which you can reach during the time. You may, for example, want to produce two pages a day.

- You can enjoy the journey.

Give yourself tea, coffee or whatever you need. Dare to take breaks whenever you want. If you dare to follow your 'inner flow' you will find that the job becomes pleasant and is finished before you expected.

- You can make beautiful finished products.

  Be a good craftsman and take a pride in your work. Take the time to make each page look attractive. You will then experience many 'highs' along the road.

4: You can finish

Follow these steps and you will complete your book. After reaching the target, you may feel exhausted and experience a sense of anti-climax. Finishing is, however, another name for beginning. After giving yourself a holiday, begin tackling the publishing and marketing. What do you do after the book has reached its audience? It may be time to look again at the list headed: 'Five things I want to finish in my life.' Climbing one mountain will reveal another on the horizon. It may be time to follow the four steps again. Take care of yourself and enjoy the journey.

HOW TO FINISH AS A TEAM

Leaders are paid to keep their hands on the job and guide their team to success. Business people live by the bottom line and know how to make profits. Ken Olsen, founder of Digital, believes it is also vital for companies to satisfy their own people. Here are ten steps you can take to reach these twin goals: to help people to feel good and to get good results.

1: You can keep your hands on the business

Janet, the managing director of a hotel chain in the heart of England, learned this lesson the hard way. Several years ago she became fascinated by total quality management (TQM) and planned to introduce it across the company. She invited a group of line managers to set up an implementation team and take responsibility for running the programme. Being a charismatic person, Janet didn't want to interfere with the team, so she gave them space to run their own show.

At first things went well. The team hired a consultant company to share their knowledge and visited several organisations that had introduced TQM. A recent survey in their own company had shown the desire for better teamwork, so they planned to start with several events to raise team spirit. Some steps were easy. The cleaners, for example, had requested new overalls and equipment. These could be given without endangering the process of TQM. The team believed that showing visible results would demonstrate the company were serious. They could then ask each work team to identify problem areas and suggest possible solutions. Staff could, for example, focus on the booking system; kitchens; reception areas; restaurants and other parts of the hotels. People could then introduce ways to make their jobs easier, improve quality and provide better customer service. The team realised this must be done in a systematic way, but felt an immediate need to raise morale. That was where things started to go wrong.

'Don't do anything,' said the consultant company, 'We have a proven system. If anything else is tried, the whole programme will collapse. First, we have to make a survey, which will take two months. Second, we will then work with you on the TQM process. Programmes often fail because of individual initiatives or other consultants advising the company. We must discover where we are in the jungle before we plot our route to the destination.'

Sounds convincing. The team were undecided because none of them had previously hired consultants. They didn't know how to value their advice; nor did they want to involve Janet, who had said it was their show. Introducing new overalls and equipment to raise morale did not seem a mortal crime, but they bowed to expert opinion. Activities were suspended while the consultants did their survey and collected their fees. Three months passed and Janet became impatient. 'What is happening?' she asked, 'I want to see some results.' The team admitted they had been duped. The consultant company had assigned a theoretical person to the account and he was applying a rigid system in a rigid way. Janet fired the consultants and took personal charge of the TQM process.

'Whatever I did we would lose,' she said. 'If I interfered, the team would feel that I wanted to take charge. If I stayed out, we would pay money for bad advice. I finally decided to step in.'

Janet's intervention was welcomed by the team. She was in overall charge of the project, but they did the nitty-gritty day-to-day jobs. She also held a two-hour meeting with them every week to look at the big picture. The team leader took over this responsibility after two months, but continued to report to her every week. She kept in touch with the tangible results and was able to ask hard questions. Janet followed the path taken by many managers who have learned from a failed project. She said: 'I realised that I must keep my hands on the business.'

2: You can be results oriented

In his book *Team Spirit*, John Syer describes two American football coaches' approach to reaching their goals. When John Madden, from the Los Angeles Raiders, asked Vince Lombardi what separates a good coach from a bad one, Lombardi replied:

> 'Knowing what the end result looks like. The best coaches know what the end result looks like, whether it's an offensive play, a defensive coverage, or just some area of organisation. If you don't know what the end result is supposed to look like, you can't get there.'
>
> After that, whenever I put something new into the Raider playbook, I always tried to picture what the end result should look like. And then I worked to create that end result.[3]

Janet didn't like American football, but she liked to reach her goal. She went back to basics by asking the team: 'What is the result we want to achieve?' They answered with one of the definitions of TQM: 'We want to involve everybody in meeting the requirements of both our internal and external customers.' Although this could be more specific, they went on to the next step. 'Why do we want to achieve this result?' she asked. The simple answer: 'We want to satisfy both our staff and our customers. We will then gain commitment from our people and increase our repeat business. This will boost our profits. How can we meet the requirements of our internal customers?', asked Janet. The implementation team knew how to begin. 'We can start by giving the cleaners, for example, new equipment and overalls. This won't break the bank, but will raise morale. It will show that we are willing to listen to our staff. After all, we want to improve our people management as well as our products.'

Good leaders often throw out old procedures and try many solutions. They cut through the unnecessary details by asking, 'What is the result we want to achieve? How can we do it?' This is a step beyond old-style management by objectives. The end result must include something about philosophy and people, as well as products, performance and profits. Good leaders welcome all solu-

> *Peak performers show grace under pressure.*

tions, providing their staff follow the company's basic beliefs and get positive results.

3: You can make sure people work hard

Sheila Cassidy inspires people to work hard in her role as medical director of St Luke's Hospice, Plymouth. She heads a team of doctors, nurses and volunteers who are devoted to caring for the dying. A devout Christian, she is a pioneer who educates the public to talk about this last taboo. She leads from the front, but is supported by staff who are willing to work day and night. The Hospice Matron underlined the staff's attitude when, speaking in a television programme, she said: 'We have all chosen to work here.' Sheila Cassidy leads a dedicated team who want to care for people who are taking the last journey.

Good leaders offer people a sense of hope and ownership. Franklin D Roosevelt, for example, inspired Americans to work hard by announcing the New Deal. Individuals believed 'there is something in it for me,' and laboured to reach their dream. Leaders must also recognise that people have different working styles. Peak performers, for example, have cultivated the internal discipline required to stick to a routine, while other people may need more external discipline. Business leaders, for instance, have to balance 'management by commitment' with 'management by control'. This is a difficult art for which there isn't a rule book.

Barrie Ritchie and Walter Goldsmith describe how business leaders have encouraged people to work more effectively in their book *The New Elite*. Sir John Harvey-Jones, Michael Edwardes and Peter Walters are among the people they mention. The authors point out that each was appointed after a crisis and go on to say:

> The same principles were used in each case, regardless of the business involved. Managing companies in crisis, it appears, is not a subtle activity. If you would like a very brief action list, it might be reduced to the following:
>
> - Sort out the cash
> - Sort out the management
> - Sort out the [staff]
> - Sort out the product
> - Sort out the marketing . . .

That is, of course, a gross oversimplification. The operative word is 'sort'. One of the outstanding characteristics of the New Elite is their ability to win the hearts and minds of the people who work for them. They believe in sweet reason rather than bullying. They pride themselves on listening first and acting afterwards. But it has to be admitted that the steel is never far from the surface.[4]

Sometimes individuals need special kinds of motivation. Per, the centre-forward, for example, usually gave 100% when playing for my football team. During one match, however, his marker kept kicking him and he retreated into midfield. We needed Per's goal-scoring talents in the danger zone, so I asked him to get into the penalty area. Ten minutes passed and he still hadn't responded, so I pulled him off the field. He asked to go straight to the dressing room to take a shower; I refused his request and ordered him to sit in the dug-out. He watched the game in silence and apologised after the match. Too tough? Per took the lesson to heart and two seasons later was scoring goals in the Swedish Second Division.

Leaders need a wide repertoire if they are to inspire their people to work hard. They may need to be good models, set clear goals, show the benefits, give reasons, create ownership, provide support, take charge, use discipline and share rewards. People respond to encouragement, but sometimes leaders must use other methods to get people to *want* to work hard.

4: You can stay close to your customers

Michael Thomas emphasises how vital this is when talking about the 'sausage factor'. After praising British Airways for their market research and attracting a large number of business people as passengers, he points out that something was missing.

For in the spring of 1983 a small airline called British Midland introduced the breakfast sausage to early-morning internal flights, and bleary-eyed businessmen switched carriers in their thousands. The supposed rationality of business travellers did, of course, demand timeliness and so on, but the added value was the sausage – the cattle truck 'shuttle' had been displaced. To BA's credit, it managed within months to launch the super shuttle, replete with breakfast, and its dominance was re-established.[5]

> *Ask yourself:*
> *'What are we*
> *doing well?'*
> *Then ask*
> *yourself: 'What*
> *can we do better*
> *– and how?'*

Companies use different methods for keeping in touch with their customers. Avis Rent-A-Car in the UK, for example, insist that all their managers, including the managing director, spend one week a year working on reception desks and washing cars. Domino's Pizza Distribution in America encourage their headquarters staff to see themselves as giving service to others in the company. The service they provide is graded on a scale from 1 to 10 and makes up part of their monthly bonus.

Leaders can stay in touch by asking their staff questions such as: 'What do our customers say they want? How satisfied are they on a scale of 1 to 10? What do they say they want in the next six months, one year, three years? How many customers do you plan to see in the next month? Let me know their responses at the next meeting.'

5: You can go for constant improvement

Two years ago I attended a meeting where a marketing agency presented their re-launch plan for a computer company. The sales director gave a superb presentation which was accompanied with attractive slides, impressive diagrams and the market divided into customer segments. One hour later he sat down after making three proposals. 'These are some possibilities,' he said. 'What do you think?' He waited for the reaction.

'They sound okay,' said the managing director. 'But I would like to know what is working for us at the moment. Where do most of our present orders come from? What are we doing well? What are our customers buying? How can we build on this market? Can you tell me these facts?' The sales director mumbled an answer, but it was obvious the marketing agency had failed to do their homework. They were in love with their own creativity and had forgotten to get to know their customer. They left without the contract.

Constant improvement is vital, especially when you are entering the last lap. Despite the fact that it appears repetitious, it is good to take two steps:

- Ask yourself: 'What are we doing well?'

Build on your strengths. When entering the last third of the football season, for example, we asked ourselves: 'What are we doing right? How are we scoring most of our goals? How can we do this more?' As we had scored over 20 goals as the result of corners, we went out and practised them again and again. This led to scoring a vital goal in a play-off game.

- Ask yourself: 'What can we do better – and how?'

British Airways, for example, conduct over 1,000 interviews each quarter to monitor their passengers' experiences. These are carried out at Heathrow, Gatwick, Manchester, Glasgow and Birmingham. Video boxes for recording complaints have been installed at major airports. The company has also created customer-first teams that explore ways to enhance service. BA's initiatives have resulted in introducing over 1,000 ideas to improve customer care.

Don't be afraid to learn from your competitors. The Japanese, for example, often steal an idea, improve it and make low-cost quality products. Ask your customers what they like about your competitors and if they want you to offer a similar service. Don't argue – just develop. Organisations that fail to do this will die.

6: You can inspire people to tackle the final challenge

Some leaders issue war-cries such as: 'Let's go for it! One more push! Come on, we can do it!' Maybe this works, but most people need something extra; they want to see the big picture. Chris Bonington's team which climbed the southwest face of Everest in 1975, for example, knew exactly where they were and how far they had to go to reach the summit. They had entered into the expedition with their eyes open and were ready to pay the price required to succeed. Bonington writes:

> Leading up to our final assault on the summit, the team had been nine days over 25,000 ft. A year of planning and effort was about to be put to the test. During our final assault, I knew that Doug Scott and Dougal Haston were intent on going for the top late in the day. It was essential to prepare the second summit team for a rescue role, should Doug and Dougal be in a bad way after bivouacking on the summit overnight. I experienced one of the truly great moments in my life when word came over the radio that the team had finally done it.[6]

Doug Scott and Dougal Haston reached the summit and the back-up plan wasn't needed. The whole team had kept their eyes on the goal, fulfilled their individual roles and knew the choices if things went wrong.

Let people know where they stand on the team's particular 'mountain'. Remind them how they built the base camp, scaled the first glacier and battled to overcome stormy weather. Be honest: say what they must do to reach the target and describe the rewards. People like to know how far they have travelled, how far they have to go, and what is required to reach the goal. They will then be ready to tackle the summit.

7: You can be good finishers

Sport abounds with stories of athletes who 'choke': those who snatch defeat from the jaws of victory. Peak performers, however, show grace under pressure. When a good football team is leading 2-1 with 15 minutes remaining, they tell themselves: 'Let's play our natural game. Let's keep being organised; keep winning the ball; keep playing the set-moves. This is when we will win the game.' Champions show their quality by being excellent finishers.

Artists have a similar pattern. One author I know takes six months to reach the halfway point in writing a book. He then relaxes and writes the rest in three months. Hence the paradox: the more he relaxes, and follows his natural flow, the harder he works. Maybe 'harder' is the wrong word. He works more enjoyably, efficiently and effectively.

Theatre groups, on the other hand, tend to work helter-skelter when under pressure. They see a visible target and pull together to get things right on the night. Lighting engineers carry out last minute adjustments, carpenters complete the scenery and costume-makers sew the last stitch. Personal rivalries take a back seat because people want to please their audience.

Some of your team will know how to reach targets, others will find it difficult. If appropriate, you can run a one-day course on 'finishing'. This can show practical ways to complete things in life, in work and as a team. Help your people to enjoy the process of completing jobs.

8: You can reach your goals

Keep right on to the end of the road. Some people finish with absolute certainty: world class 100-metre sprinters, for example, look beyond the tape and break it at full speed. Some finish with showmanship: Steve Ovett used to wave to the crowd when leading in the final straight. Some finish with a bang! Charlie Paddock, the 1920s American sprinter, used to take off three yards before the line and launch into what became known as The Charlie Paddock Leap. How will you know when you have finished? Steffi Graf realised one

Champions show their quality by being excellent finishers.

dream when she won her first Wimbledon Championship. Thor Heyerdahl reached one target when the Kon-Tiki was washed ashore in Polynesia. Dame Kiri Te Kanawa realises she has performed well when she hears thunderous applause. What are your measures? One way is to keep working until:

- you satisfy your customers;

- you satisfy your people;

- you satisfy yourself.

Getting top marks in all three areas will be a never-ending quest, so you may decide to set interim goals. Janet's implementation team, for instance, asked their hotel guests to rate their rooms on a scale of 1 to 10; but agreed that 8 would be their first target. The guests gave the hotel rooms an average of 7, but didn't reveal what could be improved. Learning from this experience, the team invited people to suggest what could be better, and provided a small gift for those who returned their form to the reception desk. Three concrete ideas emerged.

First, the TV hand-control set could be placed in a more obvious position. The design department had concocted the unfortunate idea of attaching it *underneath* the TV set. Providing one found it, it was then possible to operate the television from anywhere in the room. Hotel staff understood the system, but new guests spent ten minutes looking for the hand-set.

Second, one guest suggested wrapping two chocolates in an attractive package, writing 'Goodnight' on the outside and placing it on the pillow.

Third, the showers caused considerable distress. The mixture of hot and cold water was controlled by one knob which proved extremely difficult to master. Most guests had suffered in silence, but the questionnaire answers revealed their anger about swinging between ice-cold and boiling water.

Janet's team moved the TV hand-control set and put the chocolates on the pillow. Tackling the bathing system, however, had to be referred to the board because it would involve considerable cost. Customer ratings improved and they reached their interim goal. They still had some way to go, however, if they aimed to reach 10.

9: You can reward your people

People are motivated by different carrots, so there are different ways to say 'thank you'. Domino's Pizza Distribution offer their staff a

There is nothing more dangerous than yesterday's success.

monthly bonus. British Airways have used share ownership as a way of distributing profit. Lifeskills have a profit-sharing scheme. Some firms introduce intrapreneur programmes so people can pursue ideas which will make money. Businesses are looking to create win/win possibilities which inspire their people. Promotion is the classic way to reward people, but this must be reconsidered in these days of flatter pyramids. Digital, for example, have a career management programme which helps managers to clarify their talents and find fresh opportunities within the company. Middle managers, for instance, are a valuable resource who have lots of collective wisdom. They can be employed as mentors, intrapreneurs, or simply be helped to return to the jobs they like best. Staff win by using their talents; companies win by using their knowledge. Promotion is still on the cards but, as one author has pointed out: 'Up is not the only way.'[7]

People find that reaching the goal frequently produces its own rewards. Leaders may well, however, receive the credit for providing the original inspiration. Franklin D Roosevelt found this during his 1936 re-election campaign. People thronged his meetings, shouting phrases such as: 'He saved my home . . . He gave me a job . . . I would be without a roof over my head if it hadn't been for a government loan.' One farmer wrote to him saying: 'God bless Mr Roosevelt and the Democratic party who saved thousands of poor people all over the country from starvation . . . Life is 1,000% better since you took charge of our United States.'[8]

Leaders are only as good as their people. Rewarding them is not only moral, it can also be profitable. It inspires people to work hard for the team, which lays the foundations for building a successful future.

10: You can guide your team to ongoing success

Finishing is another name for beginning. The team may be running their lap of honour and enjoying the celebrations, but you are preoccupied. A phrase keeps going around your head: 'There is nothing more dangerous than yesterday's success.' It's time to think ahead. Tomorrow is another day, but you can start working on it tonight. Questions start to occupy your mind. What is happening in the world? What will be your new vision? How can you develop better products? How can you improve your team? What people are available? As Sir Ieuan Maddock said in *The New Scientist* in 1982:

To cherish old traditions, old buildings, ancient cultures and graceful lifestyles is a worthy thing – but in the world of technology to cling to outmoded methods of manufacture, old product lines, old markets, or old attitudes among management and workers is a prescription for suicide.[9]

The same rule applies in sport, business and many walks of life. 'Can't you rest and feel satisfied?' asks a colleague. Yes, you can, for a while. Peak performers realise, however, that inner peace and constant improvement make good companions. Companies, organisations and people must evolve to survive. It's time to plan your team's ongoing success.

Chapter 10

HOW TO CONTINUE TO BUILD A POSITIVE AND SUCCESSFUL TEAM

You can choose to develop or die. The classic sports story used to illustrate this point is that of Dick Fosbury. Before his intervention, competitors tackled the high jump by using the western roll and straddle. Few athletes do this today. The Fosbury Flop has become the accepted technique and raised standards to new levels. Like the wind-up gramophone and 78 records, the old methods have become part of history.

Some organisations must experience a crisis before they develop. Jaguar, for example, were on their last legs in the late 1970s. The standard joke then was that you needed two Jaguars: one to drive while the other was being repaired in the garage. John Egan and his team went back to basics and opted for customer orientation, quality and reliability. Far from going the way of the dinosaurs, Jaguar recaptured their market and were successful on both sides of the Atlantic. The question was: had they really learned the lesson? Had they really learned it was vital to be proactive? Or would they need yet another crisis? Only time would tell.

The Japanese are good developers. Why? Partly because they believe in continual improvement. They stole Deming from the West when nobody would listen to his gospel of quality and his ideas meshed well with those of Kaizen. They are good developers partly because they believe in making the customer part of the company. Edward Heath, for example, quotes the Chinese leader Deng-Xiao Ping as saying:

> The Americans and the Europeans come to us offering splendid goods and inquiring how much we want to buy . . . The Japanese approach is to ask us what we want, how much we can afford to pay and then produce the goods.[1]

There are five key steps in development. Let's take a look at each of them.

- Initiation
- Innovation
- Imitation
- Implementation
- Improvement

YOU CAN INITIATE

Initiators get out of the chair and start moving. As Charles Garfield points out in his book, *Peak Performers*, they 'anticipate, adapt and act'. They think ahead because they want to, not because they have to. This is the case whether they are inventing the Walkman, creating a computer or acting to save the ozone layer.

People must now take initiatives to care for the environment, because otherwise everything else would be academic. The World Health Organisation, for example, has shown that global co-operation is possible when tackling other threats, such as disease. In 1958 they launched a campaign to wipe smallpox from the face of the earth. At that time it had a grip on 33 countries and claimed over two million lives each year. Dr D A Henderson from Atlanta led a team of experts from over 50 countries who, backed by money from the USA, Soviet Union and other nations, tackled the challenge.

It worked. As John Richardson, Editor of the Overseas Association for the Club of Rome, 1982, writes in his book *Making It Happen: a Positive Guide to the Future*: 'In October 1975, 17 years after the World Health Assembly resolution, Rahima Banu, then three years old, became history's last case of Asian smallpox.' Two years later an international commission met in Dacca to confirm that no further cases of smallpox had been discovered. WHO showed how people can work together to achieve a common goal.

People must take similar steps to care for the environment; we can no longer rely on the WWFN, Oxfam and pop stars, for example, to do the job. Everybody can do something. Global co-operation, however will be needed to stop ozone damage, reverse the greenhouse effect, and compensate Third World nations for protecting the rain forests. Taking such initiatives will be a good way to care for future generations.

YOU CAN INNOVATE

Whichever area of life we look at people often ask why make the first move? Richard Foster maintains that some companies believe innovation is risky; more risky than defending their present business. Companies like IBM, Hewlett-Packard, Procter & Gamble and Johnson & Johnson have all made the opposite assumptions. He says:

> Their managers have assumed that the day after tomorrow will not be like today. They have assumed that when change comes it will come swiftly . . . They believe that managing innovation is the key to sustaining high levels of performance for their shareholders . . . They assume that as risky as innovation is, not innovating is even riskier.[2]

YOU CAN IMITATE

Don't throw the baby out with the bathwater. Theodore Levitt highlights this danger in *The Marketing Imagination*. He believes: 'We live in a business world that increasingly worships the great tribal god, innovation.' But by far the greatest flow of newness stems from imitation, not from innovation. He continues:

> A simple look around us will, I think, quickly show that imitation is not only more abundant than innovation, but actually a much more prevalent road to business growth and profits. IBM got into computers as an imitator; Texas Instruments, into transistors as an imitator; Holiday Inns, into motels as an imitator; RCA, into television as an imitator . . . [3]

YOU CAN IMPLEMENT

TAT – turn-around-time – is vital: whether you are producing new cars, television sets or training courses. Management consultants, for example, are often asked to deliver training within a couple of months. A major British transport firm, for instance, recently asked two training companies to make proposals for delivering a programme on customer service. It was a first for each firm; neither had previously run such a project.

Company A immediately asked three people – two consultants and a creative writer – to set up a project team. They stole the best from service books, studied relevant videos and asked the potential client what they required from the service programme. While the consultants designed the course, the writer produced excellent packages. Company A delivered a well-presented proposal to the transport firm within two weeks.

Company B waited until the next staff meeting. They discussed whether or not to take the project before delegating the task to somebody who was already chasing his tail. He promised to call the potential client to get more details and got around to it two weeks later. The answer was simple: 'No thank you, we have already reached our decision.' Company B put their procedures before the client, which contributed to losing the contract.

YOU CAN IMPROVE

Customers can be brought into the process of launching a product. Company A did this before delivering the training on customer service. After gaining the contract, they met senior managers and future course participants to agree on three concrete results to be achieved. Apart from agreeing on measures, these meetings also highlighted the kind of language, stories and examples the transport staff recognised and found useful. Company A ran two successful pilot courses, but still asked for tough feedback and included these ideas in future courses. They built an ongoing marriage with the customer which proved to be mutually beneficial.

Bright ideas, past glories and old technology can be overtaken by current events. Deming, for example, says companies must make improvement a way of life: this is the only way to develop their products, performance and profits. Here are ten steps you can take to continue to build a winning team.

1: YOU CAN SEE WHAT IS HAPPENING IN THE WORLD

Don't become a dinosaur. Companies can, for example, spend too much time looking inward, rather than seeing what is happening 'out there'. One morning they wake up to find the climate has changed, food is vanishing and they face a struggle for survival. Keep in touch with ideas, technologies and events in all areas of life. You do not have to embrace them, but stay abreast of the forces which are shaping the future. Here are some present trends in business and

Keep in touch with ideas, technologies and events in all areas of life. You do not have to embrace them, but stay abreast of the forces which are shaping the future.

organisations; there will, no doubt, be new ones by the time you read this book.

- rapid change;
- listening to customers;
- customising products;
- building network organisations;
- investing in people;
- managing knowledge-workers;
- quality orientation;
- results orientation;
- constant improvement;
- rapid TAT.

The first and last points have great implications for decision makers. Rapid changes in the fields of invention, technology, people management, etc., will call for flexibility and quick responses. James Pilditch underlines this in his book *Winning Ways*:

> We have to move from where we are towards this faster world, whatever the problems. It is the only way to go . . . So here we see a double challenge: first, to develop products that people want to buy; second, to develop these products far faster than we are used to.[4]

There are two kinds of TAT: one is psychological, the other is practical.

Attitude turn-around-time

This is how long it takes people to change their attitude – for example, to *want* to invent a fresh product, to manage people differently, or to save the ozone layer. This often takes longer than the second part.

Technical turn-around-time

This is how long it takes to develop, design and deliver the goods – for example, to deliver the product, to introduce a new management style, or to ban CFCs to protect the ozone layer. Technical steps can be taken quickly if the political will is present.

2: YOU CAN CHOOSE TO DEVELOP OR DIE

Stanley Goodchild, for example, realised state education must change when he worked as chief school inspector in the London Borough of Bexley. Teachers kept telling him their job was impossible, so he accepted the challenge by becoming headteacher at Garth Hill Comprehensive in Bracknell. He inherited an unpopular institution which appeared doomed. Many local parents lived in 'executive houses' and were reluctant to send their children to the school.

Goodchild tackled the problem in two stages. The first was 'image building'. As Caroline St John Brooks described in an article in *The Sunday Times*, he used the traditional English symbols of a good school to appeal to middle-class parents. School uniforms and competitive sports were reintroduced; both met with parental approval. 'The effect was magical,' he says. 'All sorts of people, from old age pensioners to bus drivers, contacted us to say how the children's behaviour had improved. One local store sent us a cheque for £500 because shoplifting had reduced so much.'[5] The second stage was to run the school on business principles. Apart from building a superb team of teachers, he sought co-operation with local companies. They were invited to make an 'investment' in the education of the students. Apple, Rank Xerox, British Aerospace, Hewlett-Packard and Jaguar were among the companies who contributed over £400,000 worth of equipment in 1988. The comprehensive now has a sparkling reputation. Stanley Goodchild has now left Garth Hill. When he arrived the school was attracting just 90 pupils a year; it now takes 210 a year and has a waiting list. He acknowledges the part played by the teachers' team and believes they will continue the good work. He has become chief education officer in Berkshire and will be co-operating with industry throughout the country. They already have their slogan: 'Putting quality into education is our business.'

Decision makers often appear to be paralysed when facing challenges. Some make things happen, others appear to ignore the facts. Why? Richard Foster believes:'The fundamental dilemma is that it always appears to be more economic to protect the old business than to feed the new one, at least until competitors pursuing the new approach get the upper hand.' Sometimes any decision is better than living in a vacuum, but courageous and *correct* decisions must be

*'We have to move
from where we
are towards this
faster world,
whatever the
problems. It is
the only way to
go. So here we
see a double
challenge: first,
to develop
products that
people want to
buy; second, to
develop these
products far
faster than we
are used to.'*
James Pilditch

made if people are to achieve concrete results. This takes us to the next step.

3: YOU CAN MAKE A NEW SWOT ANALYSIS

What business are you really in? Theodore Levitt urged companies to ask themselves this question during the early 1970s. Many took him seriously: they made fresh SWOT analyses which led to new visions, strategies and action plans.

Shell, for example, redefined themselves as being in the energy business. This led to increased research into wind power, solar energy and other fuels. Some sports shops redefined themselves as being in the lifestyle industry. This led to them stocking designer track suits, leisure wear and fashionable sports clothing. High Street banks have asked themselves similar questions since the Financial Services Act. National Westminster Bank, for instance, have positioned themselves as the bank for aspiring business people.

Defining your core business is a challenge. Liverpool and Manchester United Football Clubs, for example, might appear to be in the same business. They aren't. Liverpool are in the business of 'success'. They have achieved this goal by collecting trophies for the last twenty years. Winning is everything, but they have recently added flair. Manchester United, however, have a tradition of fielding flamboyant players who excite their supporters. They have won the FA Cup three times in the last ten years, but the Old Trafford club's lack of 'that little bit extra' disappointed many fans. Winning the European Cup Winners Cup in 1991 went some way to reconciling their older supporters. United were back in the business of achieving 'success with style'.

Keep your heart, but use your head. Ask yourself: 'What business are we really in?' Meet your staff every 12 months to make a new SWOT analysis. Build on your strengths, find out what your customers want and seek opportunities in the market. Then move on to the next step.

4: YOU CAN RE-CLARIFY YOUR VISION

Jan Carlzon did this at Scandinavian Airlines. Despite hitting problems during the worldwide recession, the company had previously demonstrated how to revive an ageing business. During the early 1980s SAS redefined themselves as being the business person's airline. Flying aeroplanes was only part of the job. Their target group also wanted punctuality, good routes and excellent service. SAS achieved this aim and made a profit. They then took another look around the world. Airline deregulation was coming and only the fit would survive. Europe would be dominated by perhaps five mega-carriers, while the rest would become feeder airlines. Carlzon's team aimed to be one of the big players. After explaining the trends in the airline industry, he told all his staff: 'The only way we are going to survive is to be one of the top five mega-carriers in Europe in 1995. Therefore our goal is to be: '1 of 5 in 95.' SAS employees now know what they must do to thrive in a competitive market.

How to create your new vision? Apart from seeing what is happening in the world, it is good to stay close to your customers. Ask them what they will be wanting in one, two or five years' time. Richard Foster believes many companies are convinced they know what their customers want. They rush in with answers, or produce products, before asking the right questions. He thinks this can lead to disaster:

> Talk to the owners of a failed business and invariably you will find them puzzled about how quickly they were forsaken by their customers . . . Even if companies do know what the customer wants in general, it's not clear that these wants can be accurately and speedily converted into the specifications for products that economically meet the customer's needs.[6]

What should be your new vision? Where do you want to be in one, three or five years? Re-visit the visioning process. Start from your destination, work backwards and clarify the 'What? Why? and When?' Involve key people in the process so they can 'own' the vision: then brainstorm your one-sentence goal. It's time for the next step.

5: YOU CAN CLARIFY YOUR STRATEGY

Scandinavian Airlines have pursued a strategy of expanding their routes to become a mega-carrier. Carlzon almost signed an agreement with Sabena which would have given SAS a central base in Brussels. An unsuccessful bid for British Caledonian, which would have given them a base at Gatwick, was followed by an approach to British Midland. Carlzon's strategy has come under fire back home in Sweden where the knives are out in case his plans fail.

Strategies should be built on your strengths. Cities such as Norwich, for example, attract large employers by advertising their quality of life. Peterborough, Exeter and Plymouth have followed a similar path. Cities that tore the heart out of their communities, a common 1960s strategy, find it harder to attract large companies. Concrete shopping centres produce a short-term gain, but they can lead to a long-term loss, if not in money, then certainly in quality of life.

What will be your new strategy? Choose the path which gives you the greatest chance to succeed: then make sure you have the skills to climb your particular mountain. The Hard Rock Café's staff in London, for example, are good at cooking and serving American food. They may or may not have the ability to run a profitable French restaurant. Make an action plan for reaching your particular summit, then move on to the next step.

6: YOU CAN REBUILD YOUR TEAM

Loyalty is contagious. Reward your loyal people and they will work even harder in the future. Take special care of those who are older. Polaroid, for example, invite staff to stay beyond the retiring age of 65. This approach is both moral and profitable. They have lots of wisdom, talent and knowledge which can benefit the company. Younger staff are also watching what happens to employees when they reach middle age. After all, they will be this old one day. They will work harder for a company that shows loyalty to its people.

Take in new, hungry people: then provide them with an induction programme. Liverpool Football Club, for example, continue to search for young talent despite being the outstanding English club over the last decade. Stars such as John Barnes and Peter Beardsley were signed to add flair to the team, but the Anfield club's success was built on recruiting promising players. These youngsters then spent one or two seasons playing in the reserves to learn the Liverpool way. Your induction programme can help new staff to know the team's goal, know the team's culture and know their role in the team. They will then be more likely to learn good habits and perform excellent work.

Some people may have to leave the team. If so, arrange for them to do so in the best possible way. What about staff who have their roles reduced? Robert Tomasko, author of *Downsizing*, believes Xerox is a leader in the field of offering such people entrepreneurial roles. Referring to their London-based subsidiary, he writes:

> Rank Xerox set up a programme for specialists in areas such as human resources, pension administration, planning, and pro-curement to trade their full-time jobs for two-day-a-week con-

Choose the path which gives you the greatest chance to succeed: then make sure you have the skills to climb your particular mountain.

sulting assignments. Long-term contracts provided a measure of security and their consulting fees for the two days came close to the size of their former paycheques. Xerox helped them to become independent businessmen, and they were encouraged to find other outside clients.[7]

Some people may be unwilling to build a mature 50/50 working relationship with their employers. They may also refuse to develop their attitudes or abilities. Give them a fair chance and try to provide a beautiful exit. If this doesn't work, you may have to be tough.

7: YOU CAN WIN YOUR IMPLEMENTERS

Teachers are being asked to improve their performance by introducing better management skills. Imagine you are the Minister for Education. You may have a new vision for the school system, but one vital step will be to win the teachers. They are the implementers who will have to make it happen. What do you know about your 'target group'?

Teachers can make school one of the most exciting places in our society. They do, however, prefer to be artists rather than policemen. Pay them properly; attract more people to the profession; and refurbish the schools. Ensure they can work with small classes in beautiful buildings. That's your part of the bargain; now comes their part. Ensure that they set clear educational goals; make learning interesting; and achieve good results. Teachers will respond to your support. They will offer students the practical tools and hope which they need to create a positive future.

Good organisations are based on the three Es: encouragement, enterprise and excellence. Encourage your implementers and they will do their best to achieve the vision. The same rule applies to the National Health Service, British Airways or Great Britain. 'That won't work, it's too soft' say some leaders. My answer is: Have you tried it? Providing they are given support, teachers, for example, will do more than a good day's work for a good day's pay. They will make things happen.

8: YOU CAN EDUCATE YOUR PEOPLE TO TACKLE THE NEXT CHALLENGE

Launch events can breed optimism or cynicism. Prepare the ground properly and people say: 'That's something we want to do.' Prepare the ground badly and battle-weary veterans say: 'That's this month's

> *Loyalty is contagious. Reward your loyal people and they will work harder in the future.*

vision.' People must see the reasons for embarking on the new direction.

As Minister for Education, for example, you may have a new school plan called 'Education 2000'. Get the right balance between leadership and ownership. Begin by listening to your customers: the students, parents, teachers, business leaders and politicians. Find out what they want from the educational system. Note trends in employment and what school-leavers will need during the next 20 years. Give the teachers a sense of ownership in creating the vision. You may, for example, invite them to create a slogan which sums up the whole package. This must be a one-liner which appeals to parents, employers and politicians. Finalise your goals for 'Education 2000.'

Teachers are perceptive, but they do not always know about everything happening in the world today. Run conferences and distribute videos to show the challenges facing schools in the next two decades. Highlight the ageing work-force and the need for life-long learning. School-leavers must develop human qualities, as well as collect qualifications. Britain depends on its human resources, brain power and teamwork for survival. The arts, for example, earn as much as the motor trade. Japan, Germany and America are pursuing one path, but we shouldn't follow them blindly. We must build on our strengths and learn from the rest of the world. Schools must balance the needs of the individual and the needs of the society. This is the reasoning which underpins 'Education 2000'.

9: YOU CAN COMMUNICATE YOUR VISION TO YOUR PEOPLE

'Live the message. Don't lead with a piece of paper,' advised one managing director. 'Live what you say before you say it; otherwise it will breed cynicism.' He spoke from bitter experience, having poured £100,000 into his company's failed launch event.

You have lived the message, however, so now you can present your vision. How do you want to communicate 'Education 2000?' Franklin D Roosevelt used his Inaugural Address to launch the New Deal. 'The only thing we have to fear is fear itself,' he said, then pushed through legislation in his first 100 days. Maria Montessori, the founder of an inspiring educational movement, used public lectures to spread her message and raise funds to set up schools. The Friends Of John McCarthy used television and the media to fight for his release from captivity in the Lebanon. Hewlett-Packard, 3M and

United Biscuits are among the companies that communicate their overall vision to their people. They then ask staff to give feedback, provide positive suggestions and report how they plan to make the vision happen at their own levels. Which method do you want to employ? Choose an imaginative way to present 'Education 2000'.

The Vision

EDUCATION 2000

The goals of 'Education 2000' are to help every student:

1 To learn the basic education skills

To learn the basics, for example, to learn to read, write and do arithmetic; to have a wide knowledge of geography, science, history, the arts and other key areas.

2 To develop their talents

To develop their individual talents – for example, to learn how to find their strengths, do creative work and finish things; to learn meta-skills such as how to learn, how to create and how to improve their own work.

3 To learn lifeskills

To become more self-managing – for example, to learn to take responsibility, to make decisions, to set goals, to work a computer, to manage change, to take care of their health, etc.

4 To find meaningful work

To find or invent meaningful work – for example, to develop their creative talents; to cross the bridge between school and work; to learn how to earn a living doing work they enjoy; to learn management skills; to learn how to work alone, in a small team or in an organisation. To be willing to re-train and continue to do creative work.

EDUCATION 2000

The rewards of reaching these goals will be:

- For the students

They will learn the basic education skills, develop their talents, be more self-managing, find work they enjoy and be better equipped to live happy and successful lives.

- For the parents

They will feel their children are receiving a good education, being equipped for the future job market and offered practical tools they can use to live happy and successful lives.

- For the teachers

They will be given the support they need to do a good job and offer their students the knowledge and tools they can use to live happy and successful lives.
They will also have increased status in the community because they will be seen as people who are helping to build a successful future for society.

- For the employers

They will get school-leavers who have basic educational skills, know their talents and can do creative work. They will also get school-leavers who are self-managing, flexible, know how to work with other people and can re-train quickly.

- For the country

They will have several generations of young people who enjoyed school, have basic educational skills, are self-managing, know their talents, do good work and can quickly re-train.
They will have parents, teachers and employers who are pleased with the educational system.
They will reap the economic benefits by having a productive work force who are also living happy and successful lives. This will cut down on the need for massive bureaucracies that have been created to care for people who have not been offered tools they can use to manage their own lives.

> *Live the message.*
> *Don't lead with a*
> *piece of paper.*

• For future generations

They will have parents who are self-managing and who act as good models during their lives.
They will learn in schools which offer an enjoyable, encouraging and effective education.
They will be given the knowledge and tools they need to live happy lives and contribute to building a better society.

Teachers will see beyond the show business. They will ask 'What's in it for us, for our students, and for future generations?' Why should they want to achieve the vision? Show the rewards at the launch event. Teachers will be given the practical support they need to build positive schools. Students will learn the basic skills, develop their talents and grow in self-confidence. Parents will see their children offered knowledge and skills they can use to find work in the market-place. Employers will get young people who are self-managing, creative and willing to re-train. Teachers who see these benefits will commit themselves to achieving the vision.

10: YOU CAN CONTINUE TO BUILD A POSITIVE TEAM, ORGANISATION OR COMPANY

Teachers are hungry to give hope to the next generation. You can offer them the support they need to do the job. Stanley Goodchild, for example, showed what teachers can do at Garth Hill in Bracknell. They will respond to your encouragement and build superb schools. They will show enterprise, produce excellent results and satisfy their customers. The rewards will be great: for you, the students, the teachers, the employers and Britain. Keep your hands on the job and guide the team to success. You will achieve 'Education 2000'.

Tom Peters and Bob Waterman have received both bouquets and brickbats since publishing *In Search of Excellence*. Critics claim that some companies praised in the book have recently hit trouble. These critics miss the point. The authors highlighted principles that businesses could follow in order to succeed. It was precisely because these firms stopped following the principles that they failed. The same rule applies in leadership. Follow the ten steps and you will be more likely to build a winning team.

Leaders are fortunate, whether they work with education, business or politics. Chris Bonington, Mother Teresa and Martin Luther King have all inspired people to excel themselves and reach their own particular summit. Whichever mountain you choose to climb, the route may appear simple, but that does not mean it will be easy. And afterwards there will always be another peak to climb in the Himalayas, Andes or Rockies. One day you may want to change your life and go deep-sea diving. Whatever you do, good luck and enjoy the journey.

APPENDIX: THE FOOTBALL MANAGER'S CHECKLIST

Here is a list of 30 things you can do as a manager when changing club or taking over a new team.

1   Get all the information you can about the club, its history, its philosophy, the backroom people who have power, the players and what people say about the club.

2   Study the team you will be taking over. Look at their strengths and weaknesses.

3   Make a clear contract with the club's leaders. Start by agreeing on the goals for the team. This may mean, for example, winning so many trophies, achieving a certain league position, playing good football or attracting higher attendances. After agreeing on this, describe the support you will need to do the job. Be prepared to leave if they do not meet this contract.

4   Build your backroom team. You may want to import people into the club, but do not neglect those who are there already. Write down all the human resources in the club. There may, for example, be people with special knowledge of goalkeeper training, medical expertise and skills they can pass on to other players. Your job is to organise these resources to help the players to develop. Many clubs have talents which they never use.

5   Sign new, positive and talented players. Make sure you have a squad of at least 14 good players and three or more match-winners in your team. The more committed players you have in the team, the more chance you have to run the team in your way. You will then, for example, be able to shed established players who want to lead the team in their way.

6   Meet the players. Win and inspire them: you must have the players on your side, otherwise nothing will work. Tell them

what they do well. Explain your ideas. Describe your goal. Explain your rules and the reasons for them. Answer their questions. Promise them lots of hard work.

7   Have good public relations. Let many people know about your philosophy and goals for the team. Inform the board, players, backroom staff, press, families, local businesses, sponsors, local public authorities. Remember: you are the newcomer, perhaps you can also learn something from other people.

8   Make sure all the practical things are organised so the players will be free from worries. This includes such things as fixing new kit and medical supplies, plus arranging the training diary, tour and matches. Take part in as many tournaments as you feel appropriate. You don't have to fix all these things, but make sure someone does.

9   Make sure the training is fun and effective. Vary it between circuit training, strength training, running, sprinting, shooting, five-a-side, full-scale matches, set plays, people playing in different positions, watching videos of themselves and in-house competitions. Ask the players what they like working on and include this in the training.

10 Make sure the players learn to take responsibility for themselves and their performances. For example, encourage them to say 'I can do better', rather than to blame the referee, weather or pitch. After building a positive atmosphere, this is the next message for you to get across.

11 Make sure the players know how to play positive football. Build on the strengths in your team and develop a playing style in which all the necessary tasks get done and everybody gets a chance to be creative. Create a simple system which is both attractive and effective. Make sure every player knows their role in the system and how they can help the team to achieve positive results. They should know how to:

- play as a team;
- play as individual team members;
- behave when their goalkeeper gets the ball;
- shout to each other;
- move up and down the field as one team;
- build attacks;

- play the set moves;
- guard against counter-attacks;
- spread the play;
- move off the ball;
- meet centres;
- make runs from midfield;
- shoot, shoot, shoot;
- behave at goal-kicks, throw-ins, corners, free-kicks and in all other situations;
- behave when the team loses the ball;
- win back the ball;
- redouble their efforts even though they are winning.

12 Make sure the players are prepared for the season: physically, practically and psychologically. Before the training matches, for example, remind them of their conduct towards referees, officials and fans. So, for instance, a warning for dissent will result in their having to run three miles the next day.

13 Play eight to ten training matches. So, for example, begin with two games against weaker teams in order to build the players' self-confidence. Follow these with three to four games against hard teams. Then play a game against super-tough opposition. Complete your programme with two matches against weaker teams. Try to give all 17 players in your squad the chance to play at least two or three games so they feel they have been given a chance.

14 Teach the players to take charge, win the ball and play their own game. They are trying to be the best team they can be, rather than get sucked into their opponents' system. The other team is just there to make up the numbers for the game. Teach the players to calm down, keep their inner discipline and keep doing the basics right. Pick players who keep working when they are under mental pressure, because they will help the team to win the vital matches.

15 Choose only positive players to start the season. They will follow your ideas, give 100% and encourage others when it gets tough. Negative players may be good individually, but when they criticise others they can make two or three team members play badly.

16 Pick the same team for three or four matches just before the season. This will give them the chance to settle into a pattern.

17 Talk with each player before the season starts. Be honest and say what they can expect from the coming season. What do they have to do, for example, to keep or gain a regular place? Let them know the standards you expect and agree on personal goals with each player.

18 Make a clear contract with the players. Repeat your philosophy, goals, rules and the rewards. Ask for their ideas for improving the club and any other support they need.

19 Ask the players to commit themselves. Get them to give a clear 'Yes' or 'No' as to whether they want to play for you. From now on you all have to pull together.

20 Before the first league match, inform the club leadership how you think it will go during the season. Tell them what you think will be the successes, crises and the final outcome. Be realistic and tell them what extra help and resources you need.

21 Before the games and at half-times, give clear and simple positive instructions to the players. So, for example, say 'Put their defenders under pressure when they have the ball', rather than 'Don't back away from their defenders when they have the ball.' Give people a clear direction they can pursue, otherwise they may feel blamed and become defensive. By now everybody should know their role, so give them no more than three messages and keep your team talks short.

22 During the games, remember that you are acting as a model for the players, be a good sport, shake hands with the opposition, show respect for the referee and officials, shout only encouraging things to your players, and congratulate your opponents after the final whistle.

23 Keep an overview. Try to step back from the game and see the overall pattern. Ask yourself: 'What are we doing well?' Make sure the team continue doing these things. Ask yourself: 'What can we do better – and how?' Try to find the patterns the team can improve. Ask yourself: 'How can I put my instructions in a positive way so the players can receive them?' Make sure you do this so that the team can improve.

24 After the games: keep your remarks short. If the players won the first match, great. If not, tell them that, while you have lost the first battle, it is more important to win the war. Give them a day to reflect on their own performances.

25 Resume training by describing 'what we did well during the game', and 'what we can do even better and how.' Make sure the training builds on each of these points. Remember it may take some time before you see the results of a particular training session on, for example, the sweeper taking more of an attacking role. Training is about creating good habits and, providing they are reinforced, they often surface two or three matches later.

26 Keep following your football philosophy. Continue to do things right, especially when there are problems. Go back to basics. Make sure people keep their discipline, start the training on time, warm up properly, practise the basic moves, encourage each other and keep working hard. Every manager faces a rebellion of some kind during the season. Reassert your authority. If any players become negative, give them a choice: to change their behaviour or get out. While making clear that you are in charge, be open to suggestions from players.

27 Make sure you get positive results. Depending on the goals you agreed with the club's leadership, this may mean winning so many trophies, achieving a certain league position or attracting higher attendances. Take responsibility for achieving these results. If you fail, take responsibility for the failure.

28 Always be prepared to sign players who can improve the team. Begin to look for players for the following season. Consider signing one or two players because this changes the chemistry and makes people fight for their places.

29 Give 100% until the end of the season, because trophies are lifted then, not during the first matches. If you are going to leave the club, make sure you hand over in a good way and prepare the ground properly for your successor. Finish the season with a bang! Thank the players, club leadership, public and press. Remind people of the golden memories during the last nine months, then look forward to the next season.

30 After the season, go out and sign the best players possible. (Providing you have educated your players to have the right

attitude, they will welcome you signing new players who can improve the team.) It is during the break that you lay the groundwork for creating a good season. After you have got all the players on your shopping list, take a break. You will need it in order to return to the pre-season training full of enthusiasm.

REFERENCES

INTRODUCTION

1 Chris Bonington, 'Getting the team to the top', *The Sunday Times*, 31 July 1988.

CHAPTER ONE

1 Lee Iacocca, *Iacocca* (Bantam Books: New York, 1984).
2 Konosuke Matsushita, *Not for Bread Alone* (PHP Institute: Kyoto, Japan, 1984).
3 Marvin Bower, *Company Culture*.
4 John Sculley, *Odyssey* (Collins: London, 1987).
5 The Foresight Group, *Second Quarterly Newsletter* (Sigtuna: Sweden, 1988).
6 For more information, see Barrie Hopson and Mike Scally, *Twelve Steps to Success through Service* (Mercury Books: London, 1991).
7 Tad Tuleja, *Beyond the Bottom Line* (Fact On File Publications: New York, 1985).
8 John Blunsden, 'Dennis confronts the difficulties of his own success', *The Times*, 7 July 1988.
9 Ibid.
10 Alan Hodgson, 'Deming's never-ending road to quality', *Personnel Management*, July, 1987.

CHAPTER TWO

1 Lee Iacocca, *Iacocca* (Bantam Books: New York, 1984).
2 Gifford Pinchot III, *Intrapreneuring* (Harper & Row: New York, 1985).
3 For more information see Liz McQuiston, *Women in Design* (Trefoil: London, 1988).
4 Peter Ueberroth, *Made in America* (Heinemann: London, 1986).
5 Robert Levering, Milton Moskowitz and Michael Katz, *The 100*

Best Companies to Work for in America (Addison-Wesley: Reading, Massachusetts, 1984).
6 Ibid.

CHAPTER THREE

1 John Sculley, *Odyssey* (Collins: London, 1987).
2 Walter Goldsmith and David Clutterbuck, *The Winning Streak* (Penguin: London, 1985).
3 Frederick Harmon and Garry Jacobs, *The Vital Difference* (AMACOM: New York, 1985).
4 John Naisbitt and Patricia Aburdene, *Reinventing the Corporation* (Macdonald: London, 1986).

CHAPTER FOUR

1 John Sculley, *Odyssey* (Collins: London, 1987).
2 Walter Goldsmith and David Clutterbuck, *The Winning Streak* (Penguin: London, 1985).
3 James Pilditch, *Winning Ways* (Harper & Row: London, 1987).
4 William Kay, *Battle for the High Street* (Piatkus: London, 1987).
5 Akio Morito quoted by Charles Garfield, *Peak Performers* (Morrow: New York, 1986).

CHAPTER FIVE

1 John Sculley, *Odyssey* (Collins: London, 1987).
2 Ian Mitroff, *Business Not as Usual* (Jossey-Bass: San Francisco, 1987).
3 UB Brands, *Focus*, internal magazine, January 1987.
4 Robert Tomasko, *Downsizing* (AMACOM: New York, 1987).
5 Chris Goyens and Allan Turowetz, *Lions in Winter* (Penguin Books: Canada, 1987).
6 Robert Tomasko, *Downsizing* (AMACOM: New York, 1987).
7 Barrie Ritchie and Walter Goldsmith, *The New Elite* (Weidenfeld & Nicolson: London, 1987).

CHAPTER SIX

1 Peter Ueberroth, *Made in America* (Heinemann: London, 1986).
2 Chris Goyens and Allan Turowetz, *Lions in Winter* (Penguin

Books: Canada, 1987).

3   Robert Townsend, *Further up the Organisation* (Coronet: London, 1984).

4   Peter Ueberroth, *Made in America* (Heinemann: London, 1986).

CHAPTER SEVEN

1   Konosuke Matsushita, *Not for Bread Alone* (PHP Institute: Kyoto, Japan, 1984).

2   For more information, see Barrie Hopson and Mike Scally, *Twelve Steps to Success through Service* (Mercury Books: London, 1991).

3   Gilly McKay and Alison Corke, *The Body Shop* (Pan: London, 1986).

4   Barrie Pearson, *Common-sense business strategy* (Mercury Books: London, 1990).

5   Tad Tuleja, *Beyond the Bottom Line* (Fact On File Publications: New York, 1985).

6   Konosuke Matsushita, *Not for Bread Alone* (PHP Institute: Kyoto, Japan, 1984).

CHAPTER EIGHT

1   Richard Norman, *Service Management* (Wiley: Chichester, 1986).

2   John Elkington and Tom Burke, *The Green Capitalists* (Gollancz: London, 1988).

3   Thomas Watson, *A Business and its Beliefs* (McGraw-Hill: New York, 1963).

4   Ken Blanchard and Norman Vincent Peale, *The Power of Ethical Management* (Heinemann: London, 1986).

5   Konosuke Matsushita, *Not for Bread Alone* (PHP Institute: Kyoto, Japan, 1984).

6   John Young of Hewlett-Packard quoted by John Egerton, 'Workers take over the store', *New York Times Magazine*, 11 September 1983.

7   Jens Neilsen, *Danish Railway Design* (Danish Design Council: Copenhagen, 1984).

8   Christopher Lorenz, *The Design Dimension* (Blackwell: Oxford, 1986).

9   George Gilder, *The Spirit of Enterprise* (Penguin: Harmondsworth, Middlesex, 1986).

10 Richard Foster, *Innovation: the Attacker's Advantage* (Macmillan: London, 1986).

11 Tad Tuleja, *Beyond the Bottom Line* (Facts On File Publications: New York, 1985).
12 John Naisbitt and Patricia Aburdene, *Reinventing the Corporation* (Macdonald: London, 1986).
13 John Elkington and Tom Burke, *The Green Capitalists* (Gollancz: London, 1988).

CHAPTER NINE

1 For more information see Chris Bonington, *Quest for Adventure* (Hodder & Stoughton: London, 1987).
2 Jean-Louis Sevan-Schreiber, *The Return of Courage* (Addison-Wesley: New York, 1987).
3 John Syer, *Team Spirit* (Heinemann: London, 1986).
4 Barrie Ritchie and Walter Goldsmith, *The New Elite* (Weidenfeld & Nicolson: London, 1987).
5 Michael Thomas, 'Coming to terms with the customer', *Personnel Management*, February 1987.
6 Chris Bonington, 'Getting the team to the top', *The Sunday Times*, 31 July 1988.
7 Beverley Kaye, *Up is not the Only Way* (University Associates: USA, 1982).
8 Hugh Brogan, *The Pelican History of America*, (Penguin: Harmondsworth, Middlesex, 1986).
9 Sir Ieuan Maddock, *The New Scientist*, 11 February 1982.

CHAPTER TEN

1 Edward Heath quoted by Alan Hodgson, 'Deming's never-ending road to quality', *Personnel Management*, July 1987.
2 Richard Foster, *Innovation: the Attacker's Advantage* (Macmillan: London, 1986).
3 Theodore Levitt, *The Marketing Imagination* (Macmillan: New York, 1986).
4 James Pilditch, *Winning Ways* (Harper & Row: London, 1987).
5 For more information see: Caroline St John Brooks, 'The old fashioned rules and high technology that saved a school', *The Sunday Times*, 4 December 1988.
6 Richard Foster, *Innovation: the Attacker's Advantage* (Macmillan: London, 1986).
7 Robert Tomasko, *Downsizing* (AMACOM: New York, 1987).

Lifeskills
Communications

Corporate Change Consultancy

Lifeskills is a training, learning and consultancy business with a leading reputation for designing, developing and delivering Corporate Change Programmes and Leadership Workshops.

Lifeskills can help you:

- Gain Commitment from the Top

- Establish the Company Vision

- Undertake Customer Research

- Train your People or Train your Trainers

- Ensure there is Continuous 'Follow-through'

If you are interested in the Lifeskills' approach please contact:

Peter Gannon, Managing Director, at 51 Clarendon Road, Leeds LS2 9NZ or telephone (0532) 467128.